ISBN: Paperback 978-1-64873-304-8
ISNB: EBOOK   978-1-64873-148-8

Printed in the United States of America

Published by:
Writer's Publishing House
Prescott, Az 86301

Project Management and Book Launch by Creative Artistic Excellence Marketing
https://lizzymcnett.com

The Genetic Make-Up Of Rebuilding Your Credit

By *Chayo Briggs*

I would like to express my gratitude to the many people who saw me through this book; to all those who provided support, talked things over, read, wrote, offered comments, allowed me to quote their remarks, and assisted in the editing, proofreading, and design.

First of all, I would like to express my success to my Heavenly Father.

A huge thank you to my mother, El Dora Bocino Lay, and father, Dr. Ervin Briggs Jr., and my wife, Dina Renae Flynn Briggs.

Then my special thanks to creative magazine, Shakeena Whitmore (*Diva Naires Magazine*), Jamila Choyce (*Courbee Revolucion Magazine*), Fatimah Sharif Muhammad, Rachel Dolezal (author, NAACP activist), *So FN Dope Magazine*, Matoya Allen (AvidXchange, Inc.), Loretta "Rita" Jones, World Financial Group, Panagiotis Lampridis Graphic Arts (Athens, Greece), Deli Rowe (R & B Artist), Eric Washington (*Fashion Trendz Magazine*), Latasha Sims (Redeemed Business And Tax Services), my cousin (actor) Rashaud Turner (Ding Up).

Most certainly, last but not least, Martha Rojas (Hermandad Mexicana Nacional), Carrie Rodriguez (Morena's

Cakes and Pies). My mentors, Monique (entrepreneur) Chang from Taipel Taiwan, Ethal Davis (CPA), Austrain Model Claudia Floraunce, and Adrian Ross (Medstar Union Memorial Hospital).

Wanda Lay (United States National Guards), Velma Lay & Milton Lay of Omaha, Nebraska, Gwenivere Lay (Management & Lay's, Paschal Family Business), Levora Lay Risper (Frito-Lay, Inc).

Table of Contents

Chapter One:

What is Credit

In simple terms, credit is the ability to borrow money or access goods and services with the understanding it must be paid over time.

According to Experian, "Lenders, merchants, and service providers (known collectively as creditors) grant credit based on their confidence you can be trusted to pay back what you borrowed, along with any finance charges that may apply. To the extent that creditors consider you worthy of their trust, you are said to be creditworthy, or to have "good credit."

How Credit Works

In past centuries, creditors might have gauged your creditworthiness by reputation. Obviously, this method was subjective to error, manipulation, and bias. These days, creditors prefer a more objective approach. In the U.S., typically they look to your credit history and record of borrowing and repaying funds, then determine whether to issue you credit.

Your credit history is summarized in files known as credit reports, compiled by three independent credit bureaus—Experian, TransUnion, and Equifax. Banks, credit unions, credit card issuers, and other creditors voluntarily report your borrowing and repayment information to the credit bureaus.

Information in your credit report includes:

- The number of credit card accounts you have, their borrowing limits, and current outstanding balances
- The amounts of any loans you've taken out and how much of them you've paid back
- Whether your monthly payments for your accounts were made on time, late, or missed altogether
- More severe financial setbacks such as mortgage foreclosures, car repossessions, and bankruptcies

To help narrow lending decisions, creditors often use a three-digit number known as a credit score. Your credit score distills the information on your credit resume to something easy to interpret, minimizing any bias.

Sophisticated systems known as credit scoring models calculate your credit score by performing complex statistical analysis on the contents of your credit file. Different models, such as the FICO® Score and VantageScore®, calculate scores differently, but all assign higher scores to individuals whose credit histories make them statistically more creditworthy than those with lower scores.

There Are Four Types of Credit:

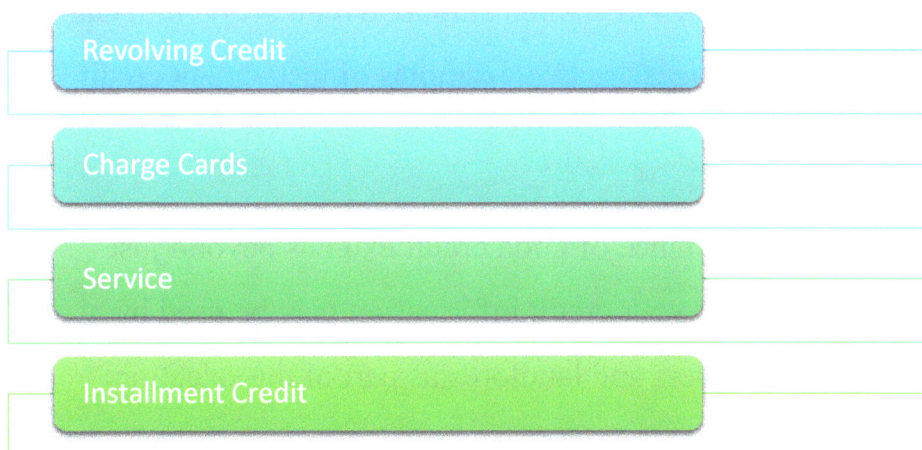

Revolving Credit

Charge Cards

Service

Installment Credit

Revolving credit: Consumers are given a maximum credit limit, and can make purchases up to that limit. Each month, the balance or revolving debt is paid back with nominal payments. Most credit cards are a form of revolving credit.

Charge cards: When someone is issued a charge card, the process works in the same fashion as a revolving card, but the balance must be paid in full every month.

Service credit: Consumer agreements with service providers are all credit arrangements. You receive electricity, cellular phone service, a gym membership, etc. with the agreement that you will pay for them each month. Not all service accounts are reported in your credit history.

Installment credit: A creditor loans you a specific amount of money. The borrower agrees to repay the money and interest in regular installments of a fixed amount over a set period. Car loans and mortgages are two examples of installment credit.

Why Do You Need Credit?

The importance of good credit extends beyond just purchases in that your credit information may be used by potential employers and landlords as part of the selection process.

Client Testimonial

"Mr. Briggs has been working hard on my credit score! I had a score of 485, my highest at about 525. So far, my score has jumped to 585. Most of the negative issues are deleted and much of the Identity theft. Getting my credit back where it needs is a struggle but I'll get there!! At least I feel comfortable knowing I'm dealing with someone knowledgeable about this business!! Very Trustworthy!!"
— Yasmin Waters

Good credit is a necessary evil if you plan to make a major purchase, such as a car or a home. Credit is a convenience that must be taken seriously, especially if you have an emergency.

Credit grantors review credit resumes and credit reports to determine financial risk. If they lend you money, extend credit, or give goods and services, will you pay them back? Your choices in life will affect your ability to gain credit. Some considerations on your resume are residence tenure, employer statistics, balances in your bank account (and whether you have an account), savings account, and the length of service. The next focus is on what kind of assets you obtain. The entire package determines whether you are extended the credit applied.

What Does Good Credit Mean?

As mentioned previously, credit is more than just borrowing money. To a lender like an auto dealer or credit card company, credit is your reputation; hence, a credit resume. It tells them how likely you are to repay the funds and fulfill your obligations, and whether you will pay the agreed amount on time every month.

Good credit means you can be trusted to repay the borrowed money. The higher trustworthiness means added opportunities. It increases the money available.

In a simple car loan example: say you have excellent credit and you take out a $10,000 loan to buy a new car. The interest rate could be 4.9% with a 60-month (5-year) payoff. This means you pay $188 each month, or $11,295 at the end of the five years.

However, if you have no credit or bad credit and want to finance the same car, the results are very different. Because of your credit history or lack thereof, you will end up paying additional costs overall. For example, if you receive an interest rate of 9.5% (or maybe even higher) over 60 months you would pay $210 each month or $12,601 in total. That's $1,300 more than if you had applied with good credit.

*The example above illustrates how credit history can affect you and should not be used as a guarantee for interest rates. *

Typical Rates, Payments, and Interest for a $20,000 Auto Loan Repaid Over 6 Years				
FICO Score Range	Average APR	Monthly Payment	Total Interest Paid	Total Cost
781-850	3.50%	$308	$2,202	$22,202
661-780	4.50%	$317	$2,858	$22,858
601-660	7.50%	$346	$4,898	$24,898
501-600	12.00%	$391	$8,152	$28,152
300-500	15.00%	$423	$10,449	$30,449

The lesson is clear: Good credit saves you money! It is typically true whether you're looking at car loans, a home mortgage, credit cards, or any type of credit.

Also, many employers look at credit history to evaluate potential employees. Your credit history may indicate your ability to fulfill your agreements, background with finances, ability to handle multiple obligations or various other factors. While employers never use credit history as the only basis for hiring, it's becoming an increasing factor in comparing or evaluating candidates.

All in all, your credit history provides a glimpse of your character, your reliability, and your trustworthiness. Start building your financial reputation today.

Chapter Two:

Reducing Debt

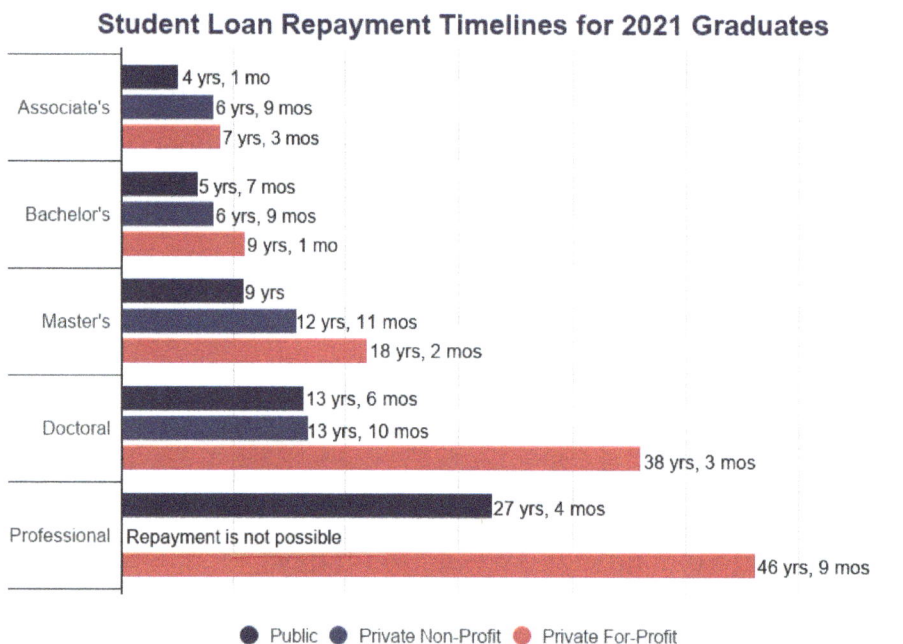

Student Loan Repayment Timelines for 2021 Graduates

Degree	Public	Private Non-Profit	Private For-Profit
Associate's	4 yrs, 1 mo	6 yrs, 9 mos	7 yrs, 3 mos
Bachelor's	5 yrs, 7 mos	6 yrs, 9 mos	9 yrs, 1 mo
Master's	9 yrs	12 yrs, 11 mos	18 yrs, 2 mos
Doctoral	13 yrs, 6 mos	13 yrs, 10 mos	38 yrs, 3 mos
Professional	27 yrs, 4 mos	Repayment is not possible	46 yrs, 9 mos

● Public ● Private Non-Profit ● Private For-Profit

Student Loans

According to Forbes, "Student loan debt in 2020 is now about $1.56 trillion. The latest student loan debt statistics for 2020 show how serious the student loan debt crisis has become for borrowers across all demographics and age groups. There are 45 million borrowers who collectively owe nearly $1.6 trillion in student loan debt in the United States. Student loan debt is now the second highest consumer debt category—

behind only mortgage debt—and higher than both credit cards and auto loans. The average student loan debt for members of the class of 2018 is $29,200, a 2% increase from the prior year, according to the Institute for College Access and Success."

But what does that mean? We all hear the reports of student loan debt and how it's out of control; therefore we must reform the program to avoid a crisis. The reality is that most borrowers are using student loans responsibly, graduate with a perfectly reasonable amount of debt, and are making a smart investment. They are given an excellent return on investment from a college education. Why is society acting like student loan debt is a problem? Instead, we should be glad so many people are working to improve their lives.

Many people fall short on their debt because they neglect to keep track of their expenditures. The first inclination is to ignore the issue, hoping it will go away. But that is the worst decision anyone can make. The fees and interest will rack up over the years, causing your debt to increase. The trick is to budget your expenses.

When it comes to paying off student loans, here are some smart ways to do it faster—before they balloon into an unmanageable amount.

1. Figure Out What You Owe

The first step to managing any budget is understanding your debt vs. income. Many young adults create student loan debt without understanding the ramifications. They become indebted before their education even begins.

The federal loan department, the U.S. Department of Education, has a website where anyone can create an account and keep track of their student debt. Plus, the college you attend has its own website to track your expenses. Once you have compiled a complete account of your debt, the next process is resolving the liability.

2. Lower Your Interest Rate

As an example, refinancing student loans— you can pay them off faster and save money on interest and fees. The first thing you need to decide is what outcome you're hoping for by refinancing student loans. There are some great reasons to refinance them: you can lock in lower interest rates, reduce monthly payments, or get rid of debt faster.

It's important to be clear on which benefits are most important. Your overall goal will dictate your refinancing decisions and help you choose the loan that will best meet your needs. This student loan refinances calculator can help you compare refinance terms and see which option gets you closest to what you want: Loan Calculator.

What is principal?

It's the total sum of money borrowed plus any interest that has been capitalized.

What is interest?

A loan expense charged for the use of borrowed money. Interest is paid by a borrower to a lender. The expense is calculated as a percentage of the unpaid principal amount of the loan.

What is capitalization?

It's the addition of unpaid interest to the principal balance of a loan. When the interest is not paid as it accrues during periods of in-school status, the grace period, deferment, or forbearance, your lender may capitalize the interest.

The capitalized interest becomes part of the principal, increasing the outstanding principal amount due on the loan and possibly causing your monthly payment amount to increase.

Next, figure out what your current interest rates are. Interest rates on federal student loans can range from just under 4% to over 7%, depending on the type of loan. Private student loan rates can be even higher, averaging around 9% to 12%.

By refinancing your loans, you replace existing student loans with a new one. It gives you a chance to shop for a lower interest rate.

The higher your current interest rate, the more you'll benefit from refinancing at a lower rate. A lower student loan rate will save you money as it charges less interest and will reduce monthly payments. The best lenders that refinance student loans offer rates starting as low as 0.00%.

3. Build Savings You Can Put Toward Student Loan Payments

Once you know the balance of your student loan debt, it's time to choose your payment amounts. If you qualified for a refinance, that's great. But now you must have the income to make the payments or the process was moot. Most banks have a savings account option to avoid monthly charges. Start a student loan savings account for repaying the loan. If you set up monthly ACH transfers, the payment can be made on time each month. Preplanning is the best way to handle debt.

Repayment Plan Comparison

Monthly Payments	RePAYE	RePAYE Remaining Debt	PAYE	PAYE Remaining Debt	IBR	IBR Remaining Debt	10-Year Standard
Year 1	$0	$207,000	$0	$214,000	$0	$214,000	$2,322
Year 2	$288	$212,273	$288	$224,546	$432	$222,818	$2,322
Year 3	$305	$217,441	$305	$234,882	$464	$231,323	$2,322
Year 4	$323	$222,501	$323	$245,002	$499	$239,503	$2,322
Year 5	$2,353	$208,266	$2,322	$232,419	$2,322	$227,793	$2,322
Year 6	$2,478	$192,169	$2,322	$218,961	$2,322	$215,482	$2,322
Year 7	$2,609	$174,375	$2,322	$206,012	$2,322	$202,282	$2,322
Year 8	$2,747	$153,954	$2,322	$192,127	$2,322	$188,127	$2,322
Year 9	$2,892	$130,663	$2,322	$177,238	$2,322	$172,949	$2,322
Year 10	$3,044	$104,238	$2,322	$161,273	$2,322	$156,674	$2,322
Total Payments	$204,468		$178,176		$183,924		$278,640

4. Enroll in an Income-Driven Repayment Plan

Even if you don't consolidate your loans, you could benefit from an income-driven repayment plan. These plans could help you avoid default or deferment, so you can continue to make steady progress on repayment. These are some of the options for income-driven repayment:

- Pay as you earn (PAYE Plan)
- Income-based repayment plan (IBR Plan)
- Income-contingent repayment plan (ICR Plan)
- Revised pay as you earn (REPAYE Plan)

5. Cut Your Expenses

A basic step to being a responsible adult is maintaining a budget that fits your income. If you are struggling to make your loan payments, it may simply be a lack of understanding your budget. No judgment here—everyone's financial situation is unique. But if you're falling behind on bills, it's worth looking at your budget.

Budget

MONTH _____ YEAR _____

My income this month

Income	Monthly total
Paychecks (salary after taxes, benefits, and check cashing fees)	$
Other income (after taxes) for example: child support	$
Total monthly income	$ 0.00

Income

My expenses this month

Expenses	Monthly total
HOUSING Rent or mortgage	$
Renter's insurance or homeowner's insurance	$
Utilities (like electricity and gas)	$
Internet, cable, and phones	$
Other housing expenses (like property taxes)	$
FOOD Groceries and household supplies	$
Meals out	$
Other food expenses	$
TRANSPORTATION Public transportation and taxis	$
Gas for car	$
Parking and tolls	$
Car maintenance (like oil changes)	$
Car insurance	$
Car loan	$
Other transportation expenses	$

- **Judgments**

If a creditor has won a court issued debt and you have a judgment filed, it is an important obligation you must deal with at once. While you can't change the past, you can improve the future. There are steps you can take to reduce the burden of judgment and improve your credit standing.

How a Judgment Creditor Can Collect

A judge may grant the creditor that sued you (called the judgment creditor) the ability to collect in several ways. Collection action depends on state law but may include one of the below:

- **Wage garnishment**

This is when a portion of your paycheck is automatically deducted and sent to the judgment creditor until the debt is satisfied. Federal law allows for a maximum garnishment of 25 percent of an employee's net wages, though

some states allow less and others prohibit this method altogether.

- **Lien**

If you own real property, such as a home or a car, the judgment creditor may record a lien against it, which will have to be paid when you sell or refinance your property. Sometimes, a judge allows a judgment creditor to force the lien, meaning you would have to sell the property and pay the creditor from the proceeds of the sale.

In some cases, a judgment creditor may be allowed to take cash from checking, savings, or other deposit accounts to satisfy the judgment. This is called a levy. Or they may levy your personal property and sell it at auction with the proceeds going toward the outstanding debt.

Depending on the state, the judgment creditor may have many years to take collection action, and can usually renew the order for another period without having to sue you again.

- **Options for handling a post-judgment debt**

After the lawsuit, you may be surprised to find that the judgment amount is far higher than the original debt. This is because the court and attorney's fees were added to the balance. Many states also allow the creditor to charge post-judgment interest as well. Because the debt can be large and the collection action severe, know the various methods for handling judgment and choose the option that makes the most sense for you.

- **Pay in full**

You can, of course, pay the debt at any time. To pay, use a personal check, money order, or cashier's check. If you must pay with cash, be sure to get a receipt. Once you have paid the total balance, obtain a Satisfaction and Release of Judgment form from the court or the court's website. Have the judgment creditor sign it, make and keep a copy of the completed form for your records, and file the form with the court. If the creditor has placed a lien on your property, they will lift it when you satisfy the judgment. You can also save your property from a levy if you can come up with the money before your assets are seized.

- **Offer an installment plan**

For judgments too large for you to pay in full, you may be able to pay in regular installment payments. Determine the amount of the judgment monthly. Be conservative—never offer more than you can afford. Put your payment plan in writing and ask the judgment creditor to agree to it. If you can persuade them to take your offer, you may be able to avoid garnishment or other collection methods.

- **Pay via the garnishments**

If your wages are being garnished, you can leave the situation as it is and have the debt run its course. Eventually, you will repay the balance this way. However, if the payment is causing a tremendous strain on your finances, you may be able to modify the garnishment by filing a claim of exemption. You would usually do this when your employer first presents you with the earnings withholding order, though you can file the paperwork at any time. The information and instructions for filing a claim of exemption are on the earnings withholding order.

CREDIT TIP

If you have outstanding debts, and are living paycheck to paycheck, applying for a new credit account might help lower credit utilization and increase your score.

If your claim of exemption is accepted, you will receive a modified order. In case you are concerned that you will lose your job because of the garnishment, know that the Consumer

Credit Protection Act protects you from being fired if your wages are garnished for one debt. However, it does not protect you if your earnings are subject to garnishment again.

Summary

Handling a post-judgment debt swiftly and appropriately is important. While you have fewer ways to resolve the situation than you did before the lawsuit, you do have options. Choose carefully and begin to rebuild your finances.

Settlements

If you have received a financial windfall, it can be a life-changing event. The funds can come from a multitude of sources. Maybe you are lost regarding the proper way to handle your future financial freedom. Do you know what to do with the money? If you already know what to do, that's good. But you still need to sit down and carefully think about what you are going to do with it before making any decisions. Remember, one or even a series of small bad moves can drastically affect you personally, emotionally, and financially.

For example, there are people who won big-time through the lottery only to find themselves losing everything and becoming more indebted in just a couple of years. Below are some ways to handle a large settlement and to know the tax consequences.

Here are some situations where you can get a huge amount of money:

- You hired the top personal injury attorneys for your legal case and won a hefty amount of structured settlements.
- You receive a big bonus from a big company for accepting a job offer.

- You receive an inheritance due to a death in the family.
- You won the lottery.

If you find yourself in this situation, you must understand the tax implications. Some settlements may be tax-exempt, but some are not. Your settlement may be subject to taxes. It is best to seek help from professionals such as CPAs and tax attorneys to make sure you pay the necessary taxes. If you neglect to pay the taxes, you are looking at higher tax liabilities due to penalties and interest.

1. Create a plan

Before you make any moves that involve using your money, make sure you create or have a plan. Ask yourself what you want to do with the money.

- Do you want to buy a house or donate money to charity?
- Do you want to fund your retirement or spend years on vacation?

Whatever your desire is, you always need to have a plan and—even better—a backup plan.

2. Hire a professional

If you receive a huge cash settlement, you should consider hiring a financial professional. Avoid doing all the investing and saving yourself. You may be saving fees by not hiring a professional, but you'll have a greater chance of making mistakes along the way.

3. Get life insurance

Life insurance is not just for you, but your family in case of a tragic accident.

4. Invest in education

Just because you receive a huge settlement doesn't mean that you should stop learning and educating yourself. I have always believed that education is one of the best investments you can make for yourself. Use your cash settlements or structured settlements to fund your education. If you already have your undergraduate degree, you may still go to graduate school and use such funding. If you don't have time to go to school full-time, you always have the option to attend part-time programs or take online classes.

Your education will not only help you personally but also professionally. This will help you as you seek better job and training opportunities as you go along with your career.

5. Invest in income-generating vehicles

When I say income-generating vehicles, I don't mean trucks, SUVs, and cars. What I mean by these are investments in the stock market, real estate, business, and others.

If you think what you received can last you for a long time, then feel free to keep the money in your bank. But if you desire to grow your money more, one of the best ways to do it is to invest.

- You can put your money in the stock market and let it grow for several years. You can invest in real estate and rent the houses you bought for passive income. You can invest in businesses and earn both salary and profit.

Just make sure you understand all the paperwork that goes with the transfer of properties.

But before you invest, always make sure that you are educated on the investments and know the risks and rewards associated with them.

6. Invest in your house

Invest by buying a house for you and your family. It doesn't mean that you must buy a big house. Buy a house that's good enough for your family. Remember that buying a house has its pros and cons. Therefore, you need to think about it carefully before jumping into buying one. When you decide to buy a house, you need to factor in the costs of maintenance, homeowner's association fee (if applicable), and taxes, among others.

7. Give back and share your blessings

You receive structured settlements or cash settlements because you deserve them. In my opinion, you'll be more deserving if you give back to your community in the form of a donation to charity or donations to the church.

Remember that donations (large or small) can make a big difference in the lives of other people. Besides, these donations can be used as tax deductions when tax season comes along.

Sharing blessings will make you feel good and help you receive more blessings financially or non-financially.

8. Pay your debt and save

To tell you the truth, it is easy to forget your debt and to save when you suddenly receive a large amount of money. Before you spend your money, make sure you have taken care of your priorities.

Pay your debt so you won't have to pay additional fees and interest. If you have balances on your credit cards, loans, and other bills, pay the balances. Without debt, I feel financially independent.

So, when you're done with paying off your debt, does it mean that you're done and can spend all the money you have? No, not yet. It is better if you stash money towards your emergency and retirement funds/accounts. Don't say that you have a ton of money to use and that's why you don't need to save. That is a wrong assumption. Your financial advisor and family can help you figure out where you need to save and what you need to save for.

Bankruptcy

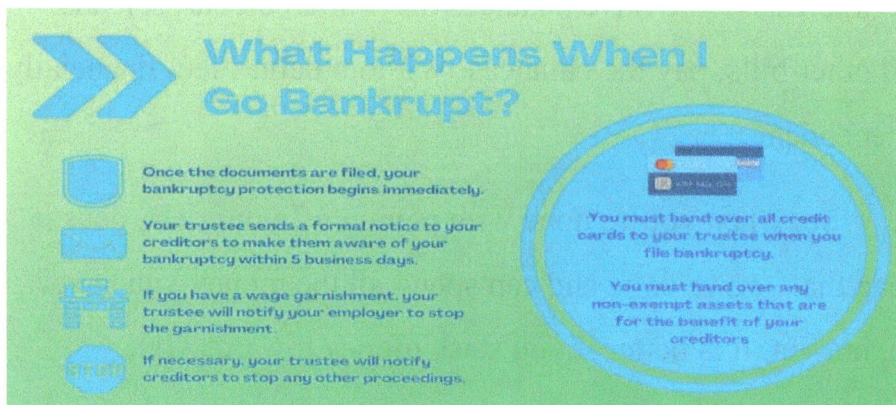

When most people think of bankruptcy, they imagine a situation where a court swoops in, takes all their assets, and leaves them with little or nothing. I'm happy to report that reality is much different. But that is the classic view of what we call a Chapter 7 bankruptcy case.

Chapter 7 is not the only type of bankruptcy available to us. There are five in total. You may have heard of Chapter 11, which companies often use to reorganize their debts. Or a Chapter 9, which is used by municipalities such as a city or a public water utility, to reorganize its debts under the protection of the bankruptcy court. Or even a Chapter 12, available only to farmers and fishing operations.

There is another type of bankruptcy that individuals use to reorganize their debts called Chapter 13 bankruptcy. Unlike Chapter 7, it does not involve liquidation. Usually, a debtor (a person who files bankruptcy) is permitted to keep all of their property, whether it is exempt or not, as long as it complies with the law. Chapter 13 may also involve more expense than Chapter 7 in terms of attorney's fees, as the process is more complicated and drawn out.

Time Commitment

Chapter 7 is a comparatively brief process and usually only lasts four to six months before the court issues the discharge. On the other hand, Chapter 13 bankruptcy will last from three to five years, or the length of the monthly payment plan you propose to the court to pay certain debts. The plan period will vary from three to five years, depending on whether your income is generally above or below the median income for your state of residence.

Chapter 7 vs. Chapter 13 Bankruptcy

The Issue:	Chapter 7	Chapter 13
Eliminate or reduce unsecured (credit card, personal loan) debt	✓	✓
Eliminate or reduce medical bills	✓	✓
Stops all creditor harassment, lawsuits or judgment collection	✓	✓
Reset utility accounts for a fresh, manageable start	✓	✓
A "home-saver" plan can be created to cure mortgage arrears		✓
Potential for second mortgages to be eliminated		✓
Potential to lower car payments through a plan		✓
A plan can be created to deal with delinquent tax debt		✓

Payment Plan

The Chapter 13 plan is simply a payment plan. It's an attempt to "reorganize" your debt over time. It's a great tool for the debtor who is behind on house or car payments. Those payments can be caught up with when using a payment plan over time, thereby saving the house from foreclosure or the car from repossession. The plan will also include any past due priority claims: alimony, child support, or recent income taxes.

The Chapter 13 plan can also include payments to unsecured creditors like credit cards and medical bills. A calculation is applied to your income and expenses to determine if you have any disposable income after all your other obligations are met. You're expected to devote your disposable income to your payment plan, and that extra money will be used to pay unsecured creditors. If you have no disposable income, that's okay; the debts will still be discharged because you've devoted your best effort to pay your bills.

Plan Requirements

The Chapter 13 plan must meet several tests for it to be confirmed or approved by the bankruptcy court. First, the plan must be proposed in good faith. This means, essentially, that you intend to completely follow through on the plan and are not attempting to misrepresent your finances or perpetrate a fraud on the court.

The proposal must meet the "best interest of creditors" test. The test requires you to pay unsecured creditors at least what they would have received under a Chapter 7 bankruptcy.

In many cases, the unsecured creditors would have received nothing in Chapter 7, so this test can often be easily met. The other practice is called the "best efforts" test. It means you pay unsecured creditors a certain amount multiplied by the debtor's disposable income.

A Trustee

Similar to the Chapter 7 trustee, the Chapter 13 trustee acts as the main point of contact for a debtor. The trustee will review the proposed payment plan and has the authority to challenge the plan in bankruptcy court if he or she believes it is improper. If the bankruptcy court confirms the proposal, the trustee acts as an intermediary between the debtor and creditors receiving payments. Specifically, the debtor makes payments each month to the trustee. The trustee then divides up the payment, as established in the Chapter 13 plan, and issues payments to the creditors.

Restrictions During Chapter 13 Bankruptcy

Chapter 13 carries a few more restrictions that are not present in Chapter 7 bankruptcy, the monthly payment plan being the most obvious. Also, you will not be allowed to incur any more debt—a car loan, for example—without court approval. You must also maintain insurance on any collateral, such as for a car loan.

Main Differences

Chapter 7 Bankruptcy

- For Individuals and Businesses
- Eliminates all unsecured debt
- Best for those with few assets
- Best for those with barely enough income to get by
- Must pass means test to qualify

Chapter 13 Bankruptcy

- For Individuals and Businesses
- Adjusts debt for repayment
- Best for those that want to keep their assets (home, vehicle, etc)
- Best for those who can pay living expenses but not their debts

Discharge

Similar to a Chapter 7 bankruptcy, at the end of the plan, most or all of your debts will be discharged. However, you may be left with debts that are not discharged, like student loans. As in Chapter 7, the discharge is personal, meaning if someone is obligated on one of the discharged debts, he or she is still liable for the debt.

Chapter 7

If you are having difficulty keeping up with your bills and thinking of how liberating it would feel to have a magic genie wish away your debt, it's not quite that simple. But some federal laws can help you manage or eliminate that obligation.

The single most common type of bankruptcy in the United States is Chapter 7. It is sometimes called straight bankruptcy. In a nutshell, the court appoints a trustee to oversee your case. Part of the trustee's job is to take your assets, sell them, and distribute the money to the creditors who file proper claims. The trustee doesn't take all your property. You're allowed to keep enough "exempt" property to get a "fresh start."

Preparation

Before a case is filed, you'll have to gather all your financial records including bank statements, credit card statements, loan documents, and paystubs. You'll use that information to fill out the bankruptcy petition, schedules, statement of financial affairs, and other documents that will be filed with the court. You can download copies for free from the website maintained by the US courts. Your attorney will use bankruptcy applications to produce them.

Broadly, these documents include the voluntary petition for relief, the schedules of assets and liabilities, declarations regarding debtor education, and the statement of financial affairs. These documents require you to open your financial life to the bankruptcy court. They include a listing of all of your property, debts, creditors, income, expenses, and property transfers, among other things. Once completed, you'll file with the clerk of your local bankruptcy court and pay a filing fee. If you're interested in finding your local court, visit the federal court locator page, choose "Bankruptcy" under "Court Type", and type your location in the bottom box.

Credit Counseling

Almost every individual debtor who wants to file a Chapter 7 case has to participate in a session with an approved credit counselor before the case can be filed. This can be in person, online, or over the telephone. The rationale behind this requirement is that some potential debtors don't know their options. A credit counselor may be able to suggest alternatives that will keep you out of bankruptcy. You can get more information about this requirement on the website for the U.S. Trustee.

Debt Management

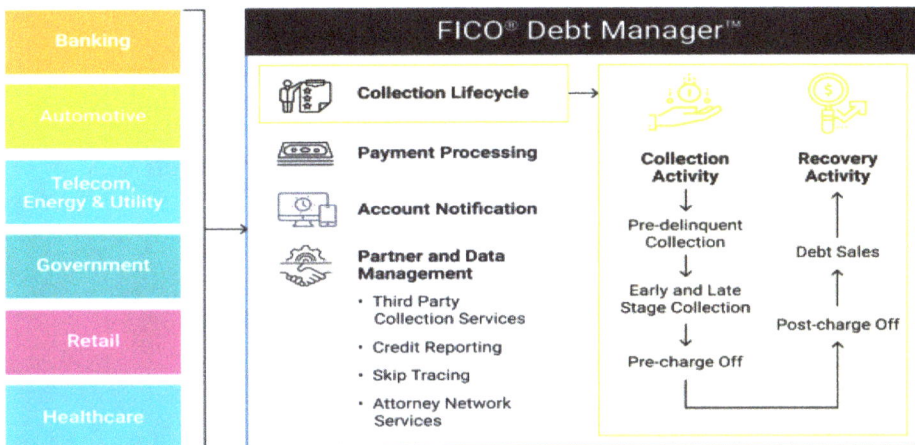

Means Test

A debtor must also successfully pass the means test calculation, which is another document that must be completed before filing for bankruptcy. This test, which was added to the Bankruptcy Code in 2005, calculates whether you can afford or have the "means" to pay at least a meaningful portion of your debts. The means test compares your income with the median income for your state. If you fail the means test, you can only file Chapter 7 bankruptcy under very specialized exceptions. Your alternative would be to file a Chapter 13 repayment plan case.

Meeting of Creditors

After a Chapter 7 bankruptcy is filed, the court will issue a document giving notice to the debtor's meeting of creditors. This notice is also sent to the creditors that are listed within the bankruptcy documents. During the meeting of creditors, the bankruptcy trustee will ask the debtor various questions about the bankruptcy, such as whether all of the information contained within the bankruptcy documents is true and correct. The trustee may ask other questions about a debtor's financial affairs.

If the trustee wishes to investigate the bankruptcy further, the meeting of creditors may be moved to a future date. It is important to note that at the meeting of creditors, as the name suggests, any creditor may appear and ask a debtor questions about their bankruptcy and finances. In reality, however, the only creditors who appear regularly are car creditors (to ask what you intend to do about your car payments) and the IRS (to ask when you're going to pay back those non-dischargeable taxes).

Seizure of Assets

If you have any non-exempt property, the bankruptcy trustee can seize and sell the property. Exemptions refer to federal or state statutes that allow you to protect certain types of property when you file bankruptcy. For example, exemptions exist to protect retirement accounts such as a 401(k) plan. Any assets that the trustee can recover are distributed to creditors.

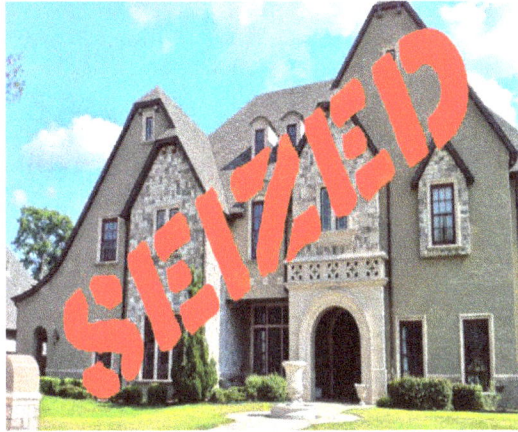

Financial Management Course

Before most debtors can receive a discharge, they will have to take a course in financial management. This class is likely taught by the same group that you used for credit counseling. Plan to spend about one and a half hours in person, online, or on the telephone.

Discharge

A bankruptcy discharge **relieves the borrower** from their legal obligation to pay certain debts.

Source: United States Courts

If the trustee and the creditors do not object to the debtor's discharge, the bankruptcy court will automatically give the debtor a discharge at some point after the last day to object. The last day to file a complaint objecting to a debtor's discharge is 60 days after the first session of the meeting of creditors. If no complaint is filed, the discharge is usually entered several days later. The discharge prevents creditors from attempting to collect any debt against you personally that arose before the filing of the bankruptcy.

Thus, the discharge effectively wipes out debts. However, it is important to note that not all debts are dischargeable, including certain taxes and child or spousal support obligations. Furthermore, a discharge is personal. This means that a creditor can still collect on a discharged debt from a co-debtor that did not file for bankruptcy. A creditor with collateral may also be able to use that collateral to satisfy some of the outstanding debt.

What is Liquidated Debt?

Have you ever wondered whether you owe a creditor a certain amount of money? Have there ever been instances where you just weren't sure if you'd been charged, or whether your payment had been accepted, or even if you were responsible for a debt?

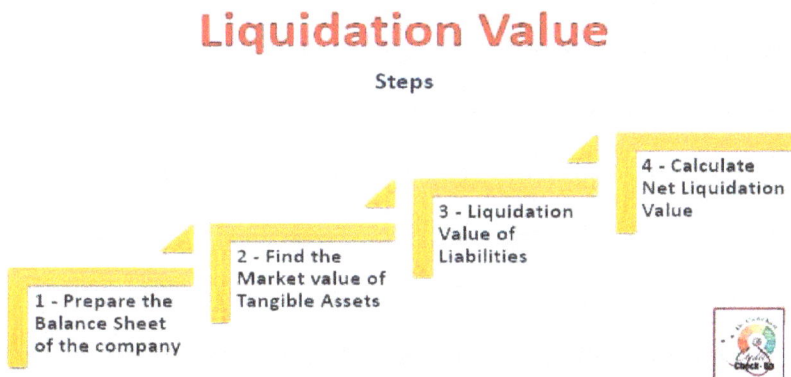

Liquidation Value

Steps

4 - Calculate Net Liquidation Value

3 - Liquidation Value of Liabilities

2 - Find the Market value of Tangible Assets

1 - Prepare the Balance Sheet of the company

For many debts, it's not hard to figure out what you owe. Your creditor makes it easy for you by sending a statement—usually monthly—outlining your charges, the interest that's accrued, any fees you've incurred, payments you made during the billing cycle, and your balance.

In certain situations, some accounts have outstanding balances, and you may be unable to determine the amount that is owed.

These are called liquidated debts. When the balance owed is certain, an agreement can be determined by the borrower and lender in terms of a contract or possibly from a legal proceeding.

Unliquidated vs. Disputed or Contingent Debt

Closely related to the concept of liquidated debt is disputed and contingency debt.

A debt is disputed when some element of the contract or agreement between the parties is unclear. One party may deny that it has any responsibility for the debt at all. The borrower may dispute the balance because they haven't gotten credit for payments they have made.

A debt is contingent if some event must occur before the debtor becomes liable for the debt. A common example is a guarantor. The guarantor agrees to pay the debt, but only if the primary borrower defaults—doesn't pay, or otherwise fails to meet the terms of the agreement.

Debt can be unliquidated, disputed, or contingent, and it can be two of those or all three.

TIMELINE OF A CHAPTER 7 FILING

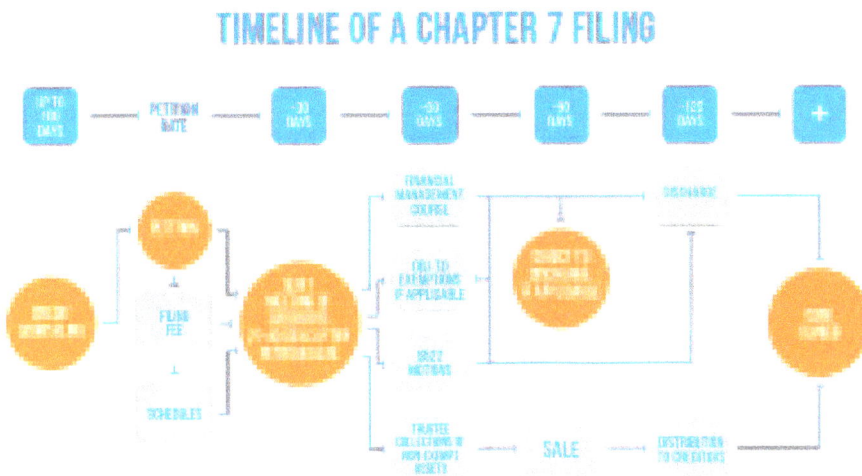

Liquidated Debts in Bankruptcy

The status of debt is important in the context of a bankruptcy case. Debts have to be certain, or liquidated, before a bankruptcy trustee can pay a claim. Likewise, there must be no dispute or contingency pending.

Examples of Liquidated and Unliquidated Debt

Here are some examples of liquidated and unliquidated debt. Debt can arise from many sources. For our purposes, let's consider torts, which are civil wrongs that cause damage to others or the property of others. We'll also look at the debt that arises from the contract.

Liquidated Tort Debt

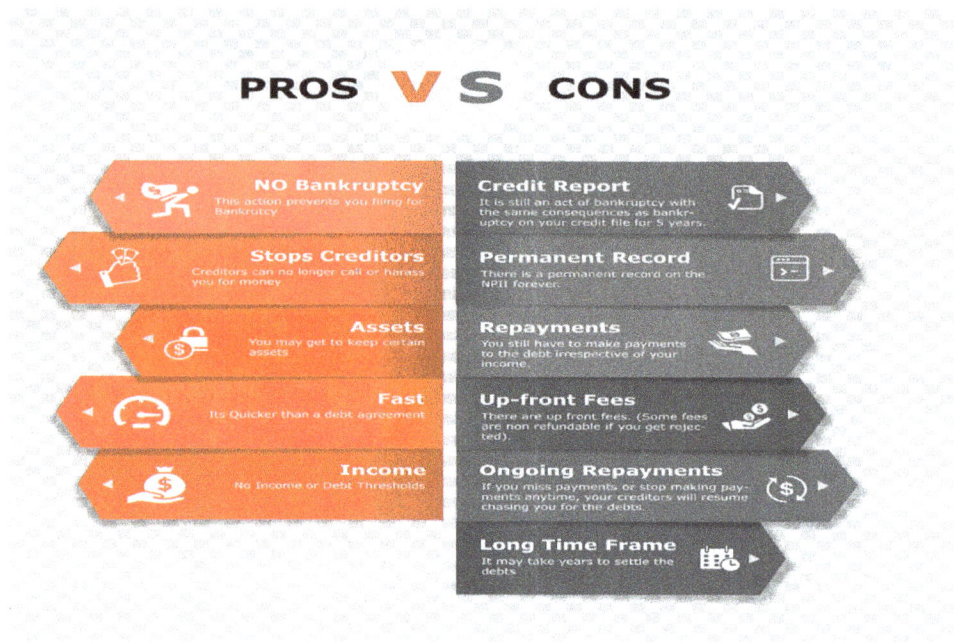

PROS VS CONS

PROS	CONS
NO Bankruptcy This action prevents you filing for Bankrutcy	**Credit Report** It is still an act of bankruptcy with the same consequences as bankruptcy on your credit file for 5 years.
Stops Creditors Creditors can no longer call or harass you for money	**Permanent Record** There is a permanent record on the NPII forever.
Assets You may get to keep certain assets	**Repayments** You still have to make payments to the debt irrespective of your income.
Fast Its Quicker than a debt agreement	**Up-front Fees** There are up front fees. (Some fees are non refundable if you get rejected).
Income No Income or Debt Thresholds	**Ongoing Repayments** If you miss payments or stop making payments anytime, your creditors will resume chasing you for the debts.
	Long Time Frame It may take years to settle the debts

The Car Accident, Part 1: During rush hour one afternoon, someone rear-ended you, and you rear-ended the car in front. The driver ahead had to be taken to the hospital. After treatment and getting an estimate on fixing his car, the driver was out $4,379. He knows exactly how much because he's got in bills and the estimate to prove it. Unless you have some reason to dispute the amount, the $4,379 is a liquidated debt.

The Car Accident, Part 2: Let's say that the driver suffered an injury that will require treatment for an extended period. Until that treatment is completed, the amount of the debt is unliquidated because no one knows exactly how much it will take to make the driver whole again, if at all. But if you are found liable for the accident, you can agree to pay a certain sum to the driver and be released from any future responsibility for payments. Then the debt is liquidated because the parties have agreed.

The Car Accident, Part 3: So instead of agreeing with the driver, let's say you dispute either how much you owe, or whether you're even liable for the accident (after all, someone rear-ended you first). The injured driver takes you to court and the judge or the jury finds that: 1. You caused the driver's injuries, and 2. You owe the driver $50,000. Because the court enters a judgment for a certain sum, the debt you owe is liquidated.

The situation can apply to similar situations. For example, your dog bites a neighbor. The neighbor sues you for defamation and lying about the bite on social media. You spray paint "dog hater" on your neighbor's fence. You get the picture.

Liquidated Contractual Debt

The Car Loan unliquidated debts aren't limited to accident situations; they can also occur when a contract is involved. For instance, you borrowed money to buy a car and you have a contract that requires you to pay $300 per month for

36 months for a total of $10,800. I would argue that the amount is liquidated. But after some time you acquire enough money to pay off the loan early. The amount paid is $9,500. That, too, is a liquidated amount, because it's easily calculated. You and the lender both agree to the balance owed.

Consider what happens when you lose your job and can't make the payments anymore. The lender repossesses your car and puts it up for sale. If the lender doesn't get enough from the sale to pay off your debt, you'll be liable for the difference. But, until the car is sold, the debt is unliquidated. The final account balance cannot be determined.

It's possible, although highly unlikely, that the sale will bring in enough to pay the loan in full. So, the contingency is whether or not the sale pays off the loan.

Bankruptcy Exemptions: Schedule C

Choosing your exemptions is critical to what property you keep after bankruptcy.

One of the purposes of our bankruptcy system is to give people who have had financial issues a "fresh start." To that end, no bankruptcy is going to leave a debtor destitute. The debtor and his or her dependents will always be left with the basics for a new start. That will include furniture, clothing, household goods, cars, and equity in a homestead.

The property that you're allowed to keep in a bankruptcy case is called exempt property. The court and your creditors must know what property you intend to keep, and the bankruptcy code requires that you affirmatively claim those exemptions.

Where Do You Find Exemptions?

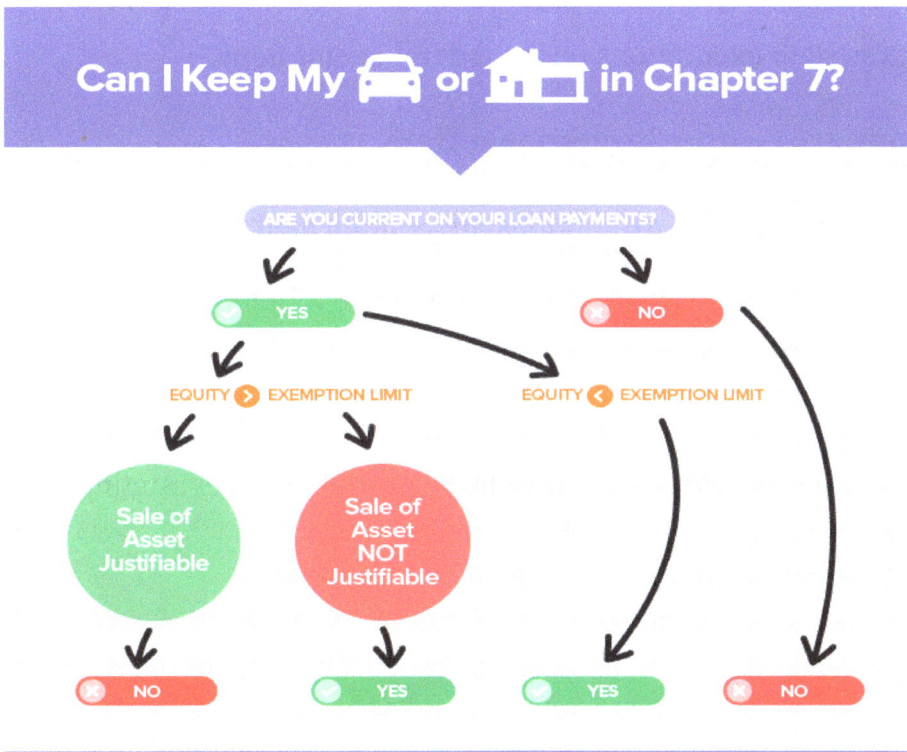

Can I Keep My 🚗 or 🏠 in Chapter 7?

ARE YOU CURRENT ON YOUR LOAN PAYMENTS?

YES — NO

EQUITY > EXEMPTION LIMIT — EQUITY < EXEMPTION LIMIT

Sale of Asset Justifiable — Sale of Asset NOT Justifiable

NO — YES — YES — NO

Bankruptcy exemptions are based on state and federal law, and each state has enacted its exemptions. These exclusions apply to more than just bankruptcy cases; they also apply when a creditor obtains a judgment and wants to take property from the debtor to satisfy an account.

Congress has also passed a set of federal exemptions. Depending upon where you live and file for bankruptcy, the law of the state may permit you to only use the state exemptions, as opposed to the federal exemptions. For example, in California, you may only choose state exemptions and not federal exemptions. But in Texas, you can choose whether to apply the Texas state exemptions or the federal exemptions.

Consider Getting Professional Help

Bankruptcy exemptions are complicated. Although you don't have to hire an attorney to represent you during the bankruptcy case, it is very important to have assistance when you choose your exemption list. If you get it wrong, the consequences can range from uncomfortable to devastating.

Bankruptcy Schedule C

One of the documents you file with your bankruptcy paperwork is called Schedule C: The Property You Claim as Exempt, Official Form B 106C. Schedule C is arguably the most important document that you complete when filing for bankruptcy, no matter the chapter. Schedule C contains your claims of exemption. These exemptions permit you to keep property that would otherwise become the property of the bankruptcy estate and the bankruptcy trustee.

Completing Schedule C

Part 1, Question 1

In Part 1 of Schedule C, you will notice that the document requires you to select a box if you are claiming exemptions according to 11 U.S.C. section 522(b)(2) or 11 U.S.C. section 522(b)(3). If you choose state law exemptions, select 522(b)(3); section 522(b)(2) indicates that you have chosen federal law exemptions. Some states do not allow you to choose federal law exemptions. Consult with a bankruptcy lawyer to determine if this is the case in your state of residence.

Part 1, Question 2

Description of Property

Starting with Question 2, you will list all of the property from Schedule A/B for which you claim an exemption. If you do not list property from Schedule A/B it will not be exempt, and the bankruptcy trustee may take it and sell it! You should use the same descriptions that you used in Schedule A/B.

Current Value of the Portion You Own

You will also state the current value of the portion of the property that you own. You can choose to list a specific amount. For example, in California, section 703.140(b)(3) allows residents to claim up to $550 per item. Thus, in that example, you would put $550 in the blank for the value. As an alternative, you can choose to say that you are claiming 100% of the fair market value and up to any limits listed in the applicable exemptions statute you are using.

Specific Laws that Allow Exemption

In this section, you will put the specific code section that provides for the exemption. For example, in California, you would cite California Code of Civil Procedure section 703.140(b)(3) for exemptions in household goods and clothing. Each state has its own set of exemptions, and there are immunities contained in the bankruptcy code and other federal statutes.

For more, see Bankruptcy Exemptions By State.

Part 1, Question 3

You will be asked if you are claiming an exemption in your homestead of more than a certain amount (which adjusts every three years), and whether you acquired the property more than 1,215 days before you filed the bankruptcy case. You are limited to a homestead exemption of a certain maximum amount if you obtained the homestead relatively recently. This is to prevent filers from converting non-exempt assets into cash and using that cash to purchase an expensive property not long before filing bankruptcy.

Part 2

The second page is just a continuation of Part 1, Question 2. You can also add additional pages as necessary to ensure that you have covered all property you wish to exempt.

Objections to Your Claims of Exemption

After you file your bankruptcy, any creditor, the bankruptcy trustee, or the U.S. Trustee can object to your claims of exemption. This is done by filing a written objection with the bankruptcy court. A hearing will be conducted before a bankruptcy judge on the objection. A party may object to your claims of exemption for a variety of reasons, such as improperly categorized exemptions (claiming an exemption in clothes under an exemption statute for a car). An objection to your claims of exemption must be filed within 30 days after the trustee concludes your meeting of creditors, or within 30 days of any amendments to Schedule C.

Allowance of Exemptions

If no one objects to your exemptions within the above-referenced 30-day period, your exemptions will be allowed by "operation of law." This means that your exemptions are automatically allowed and you don't have to be concerned that the trustee will come after any property that you've exempted.

Secured Credit

Secured credit cards can help people with bad credit or short credit histories fix this situation. Here's what you need to know to understand secured cards and how they differ from regular unsecured cards.

What is a Secured Credit Card?

A secured credit card is backed by a cash deposit you make when you open the account. The deposit is usually equal to your credit limit. So, if you deposit $200, you'll have a $200 limit.

The deposit reduces the risk to the credit card issuer. If you don't pay your bill, the issuer can take the money from your deposit. That's why these cards are available to people with bad credit or no credit.

What happens to that $200 deposit if you always pay your bill on time? You'll eventually get it back. Use the card responsibly, and you can improve your credit enough to qualify for an unsecured card—one that doesn't require a deposit.

Some cards may allow you to upgrade your account directly to an unsecured card. Others don't have an upgrade process, so you'll have to apply elsewhere, then close the secured card. When you upgrade or close a non-delinquent secured card, the issuer refunds your deposit.

The minimum and maximum amount you can deposit varies by card, but you should be prepared to come up with at least $200 for a secured card deposit.

Secured vs. Unsecured Cards

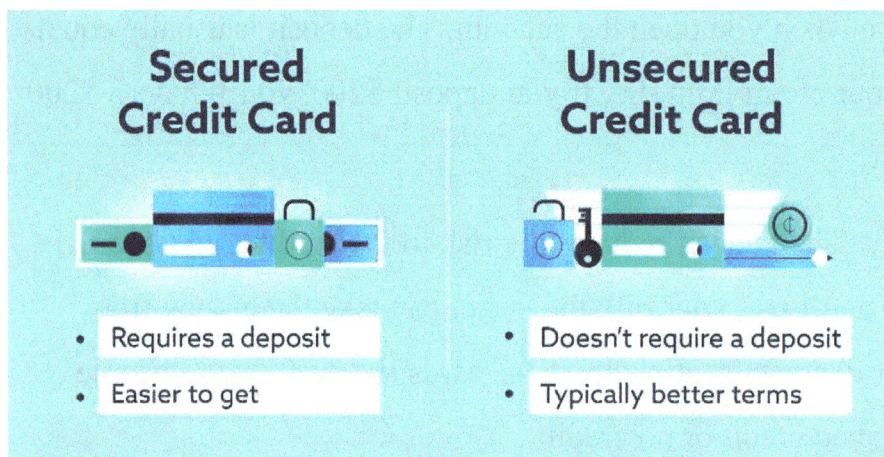

Secured Credit Card
- Requires a deposit
- Easier to get

Unsecured Credit Card
- Doesn't require a deposit
- Typically better terms

Whether you need a secured card comes down to how good your credit is.

For unsecured cards, which don't require a deposit and therefore pose more risk to the issuer, credit card companies typically require at least average credit, and good or excellent credit for the best ones.

Some unsecured credit cards advertise themselves as easy to qualify for even if you have bad credit. But these cards usually charge extremely high fees. I recommend a secured card rather than a high-fee unsecured card.

How Secured Credit Cards Work?

Once the initial deposit is paid, secured cards work just like unsecured ones.

- You can use them wherever credit cards are accepted, including online.
- You can build or rebuild your credit by using the card responsibly and paying your balance on time.
- You incur interest if you carry a balance.

Most major credit card issuers offer both secured and unsecured cards. Annual fees are common, but you shouldn't pay more than $50. You can find secured cards with a $0 annual fee among our favorites.

If you can't qualify for an unsecured card, a secured card can be a great tool as you look to improve your credit. But it's as important to be responsible with a secured card as it is with any other loan or bill that shows up on your credit report.

Secured Credit Cards vs. Prepaid Debit

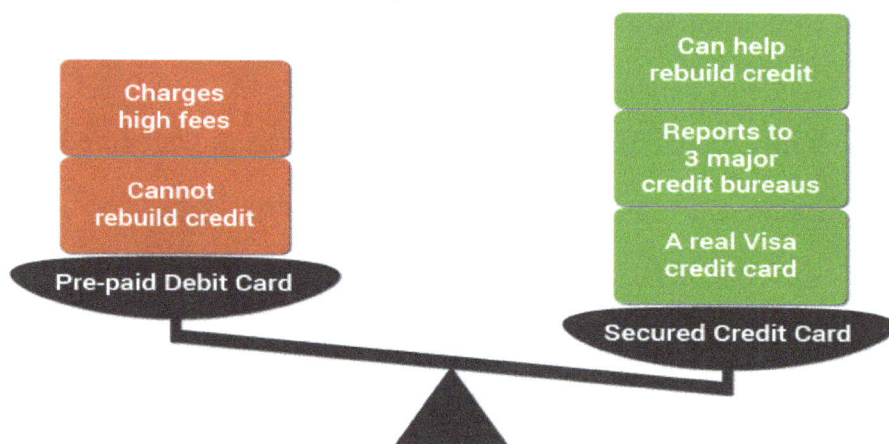

Prepaid debit cards seem similar to secured credit cards. You have to pay money before you can use the card, and they typically have a Visa, MasterCard, or American Express logo.

But with prepaid debit cards, you're using your own money to make purchases—not money borrowed from the issuer. You load money onto the card, then the issuer uses that money to pay for your purchases.

If building credit is your goal, a secured credit card is a better bet than a prepaid card. Since these cards don't extend any credit, account activity isn't reported to the credit bureaus. Therefore, you're not building a credit history by using a prepaid card. Prepaid debit cards can also have fees that secured credit cards do not.

How to Use a Secured Card Effectively?

Although they require a deposit, secured credit cards are a powerful tool for rebuilding credit. Here's how to use one most effectively:

- Use the card sparingly, making only one or two small purchases every month.
- Pay your balance in full every month before the due date. When you pay in full, you won't be charged interest. Interest rates on secured cards are generally higher than those on unsecured cards.

Keep an eye on your credit score over time; when it has meaningfully improved, ask your issuer about upgrading to an unsecured card

Many people find that by using a secured card carefully, it takes only about a year to improve their credit score enough that they're able to qualify for an unsecured card. Some issuers will let you transfer your secured line of credit to an unsecured one, which is better for your credit score because it doesn't require you to open a new account.

But even if you do have to apply for a new unsecured credit card, you may be able to enjoy some of the benefits of having good credit—lower interest, rewards, and more competitive fees. When that day comes, your time rebuilding your credit with a secured credit card will have been worth it.

Auto Loans

Shopping for the lowest interest rate on your auto loan before you buy your next car puts you in a stronger negotiating position and saves you money over the life of your loan. If you already have a loan, you may be able to lower your monthly payment and save money by refinancing your car loan. Find your best interest rate by comparing multiple auto loan offers.

What to Know Before You Apply

Interest rates: The interest rate you'll get depends on your credit score and income, the length of the loan you choose, and the vehicle. If you have a loan and make consistent, on-time payments, your credit score will improve and you may be able to refinance your car loan to get a better rate and lower your monthly payment.

Loan terms: Some lenders offer loans for up to 84 months. However, it's best to pay off a car loan quickly since cars depreciate rapidly. Owing more on the loan than the car is worth is called being "underwater" or "upside down," which is a risky financial situation. Also, the best interest rates are available for shorter loan terms. We recommend 60 months for new cars and 36 months for used cars.

"Soft" vs. "hard" credit pull:

⭕ Hard Inquiry

Also referred to as a Hard Pull. Happens when you apply for credit card, loans, or mortgage. Can affect your credit score by approximately 5 points an stay there for 6 months.

⭕ Soft Inquiry

Also referred to as Soft Pull. Happens when your credit report is checked for a background or by a mortgage lender for pre-approval. Doesn't affect your credit score.

Some lenders do a "soft pull" of your credit to pre-qualify you for a loan. This doesn't damage your credit score, but it also doesn't guarantee you'll be approved for a loan or get the exact rate you're quoted. Other providers run a full credit check, which temporarily lowers your credit score by a few points. But again, your final rate could differ slightly from your preapproval quote. A hard pull will be required in all cases before a loan is finalized.

Rate shopping: Applying to several lenders helps you find the most competitive interest rate. However, it can lead to you being contacted by multiple lenders, or even dealers when you apply for a purchase loan, especially if you use a service that compares offers for you (such as myAutoloan).

If you worry that your credit score could keep you from buying a car, you underestimate how much car dealers want to sell you one. But remember, a higher score will almost certainly get you a lower interest rate.

At the end of 2020, the average credit score for a new car loan was 713, and 656 for a used car loan, according to an Experian report.

But nearly 20% of car loans go to borrowers with credit scores below 600, according to Experian. Almost 4% go to those with scores below 500.

Car Loan Rates by Credit Score

Someone with a score in the low 700s might see rates on used cars of about 5%, compared with 15% or more for a buyer with a score in the mid-500s, according to data provided by Experian.

On a $20,000 five-year loan, that's a monthly payment of $483 compared with $378 for the buyer with better credit. Plus, in most states, bad credit can mean much higher car insurance rates too.

Credit score	Average new-car APR	Average used-car APR
781-850	3.23%	3.95%
661-780	4.16%	5.68%
601-660	7.05%	10.44%
501-600	11.35%	16.92%
300-500	14.07%	19.81%

Source: State of the Automotive Finance Market, Experian Information Solutions Inc.

What to Expect in the Finance Office?

If you're concerned about approval, prepare by focusing on the positives in your financial life. Remember, people with major blemishes on their credit are routinely approved for car loans. For example, someone who has a low score from a business debt but hasn't missed a car payment in 20 years may be approved. You're also more likely to get financing if you have a stable job, own a home, and/or put down a substantial down payment.

Before You Go Shopping

It's smart to have some idea of what dealers will see when they check your credit profile.

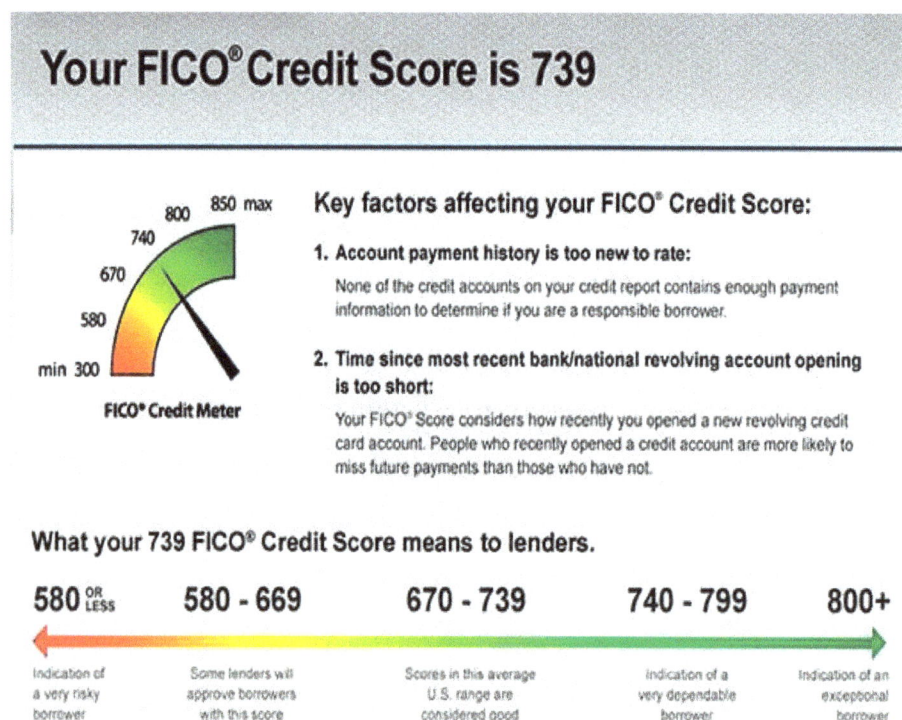

Your FICO® Credit Score is 739

FICO® Credit Meter

800   850 max
740
670
580
min 300

Key factors affecting your FICO® Credit Score:

1. **Account payment history is too new to rate:**

   None of the credit accounts on your credit report contains enough payment information to determine if you are a responsible borrower.

2. **Time since most recent bank/national revolving account opening is too short:**

   Your FICO® Score considers how recently you opened a new revolving credit card account. People who recently opened a credit account are more likely to miss future payments than those who have not.

What your 739 FICO® Credit Score means to lenders.

580 OR LESS	580 - 669	670 - 739	740 - 799	800+
Indication of a very risky borrower	Some lenders will approve borrowers with this score	Scores in this average U.S. range are considered good	Indication of a very dependable borrower	Indication of an exceptional borrower

A free score, so long as it's on a 300-to-850 scale, is likely to give you a rough idea of where you stand so you aren't disappointed if you don't get an advertised interest rate.

You can also buy your FICO automotive score through the company website. That score gives more weight to how you have repaid car loans in the past.

Many lenders use auto-specific credit scores that weigh past car loan payments more heavily.

If you have time to delay your car purchase, work on improving your credit. That means:

➢ Paying every bill on time, every time
➢ Keeping credit card balances low relative to credit limits
➢ Avoid applying for other credit within 6 months of applying for a car loan
➢ Keeping old credit cards open unless there's a compelling reason to close them

If you've already signed the dotted line on a higher-rate loan, keep an eye on your scores. You may be able to refinance your auto loan at a lower rate after you've made on-time payments for six to 12 months.

Restrictions: Some lenders only work with a network of dealerships. Others won't lend money to buy cars from private sellers. Lenders may also exclude some makes of cars, certain models, and types of vehicles, such as electric cars.

Funding: Once the loan is finalized, the lender will offer you a loan with a maximum amount at a stated interest rate. For purchase loans, lenders provide the money in a variety of ways: a no-obligation check, direct deposit to your bank account, or a certificate to be used at a car dealership. For auto refinance loans, the lender typically pays off your old lender and you begin making payments to the new lender.

Mortgage Loans

Required Documents for Your Application

Before starting your application, you'll want to have the correct information on hand to help the process run smoothly:

- A copy of your most recent YTD pay stub(s)

- Signed business and personal tax returns from the past two years

- W-2 statements from the past two years

- For those self-employed, a copy of the most recent quarterly or year-to-date profit/loss statement

- Two recent bank statements for all financial accounts such as checking, savings, IRA, and 401(k)

- Most recent monthly statements for any mortgages

- Social Security card and valid driver's license

Additional documents may need to be provided depending on the type of loan for which you are applying.

As the U.S. economy continues to rebuild from the recession that happened almost nine years ago, lots of people are looking to buy homes after years of renting or staying put in a previous house. As a result, the real estate market is competitive in many parts of the country, requiring buyers to put in aggressive offers and, in some places, compete with deep-pocketed investors paying in cash.

What this means is that—now more than ever—you need to be qualified for a mortgage before you shop for real estate.

Understanding Today's Mortgage Market

Before the housing crisis of 2008-09, it seemed that anybody with a pulse could get a mortgage (or two or three). Lenders pushed "sub-prime" loans on people with poor credit, knowing the entire time that the applicants couldn't afford the payments and would eventually default.

These lending habits were unsustainable, and we know the rest of the story. The banks got bailouts while millions of homeowners either lost their homes or got stuck underwater (owing much more on their mortgage than their home was worth).

Even as the real estate market begins to recover, the mortgage crisis has left its mark. Mortgage underwriting—the criteria banks use to determine whether to make a loan—is more stringent. That's not to say that young couples or other first-time homebuyers will have a difficult time getting a mortgage. But it means that proving to the bank that you're financially prepared for a mortgage is more important than ever.

What it Takes to Get Approved for a Mortgage

Before completing a mortgage application or even strolling through an open house, you'll want to know these things:

Your monthly income

> ➤ The sum of your total monthly debt payments: auto loans, student loans, and credit card minimum payments

> ➤ Your credit score and any credit issued in the past few years
>
> ➤ How much cash you can put down?
>
> ➤ How much house you can afford (use our simple calculator to estimate this)

1. Calculate your income and your monthly debt obligations

The first step in preparing to apply for a mortgage is to document your monthly income and debt payments. You'll need to provide at least two weeks of pay stubs to your lender, so it doesn't hurt to start collecting those. If you're self-employed or have variable income, expect the underwriting process to be a bit more involved. You may, for example, have to submit copies of your past one or two tax returns. The lender may then count the average of your last two year's income or the lower of the two numbers.

Getting approved for the mortgage you want is all about staying within certain ratios lenders use to determine how much you can afford for a mortgage payment. Large debt payments (an auto loan or big student loans) will limit the size of the mortgage approval you can get. If possible, pay these loans off or, at the very least, avoid taking any new loan payments.

2. Give your credit health a checkup

Before applying for a mortgage, obtain both your credit score and your credit history report.

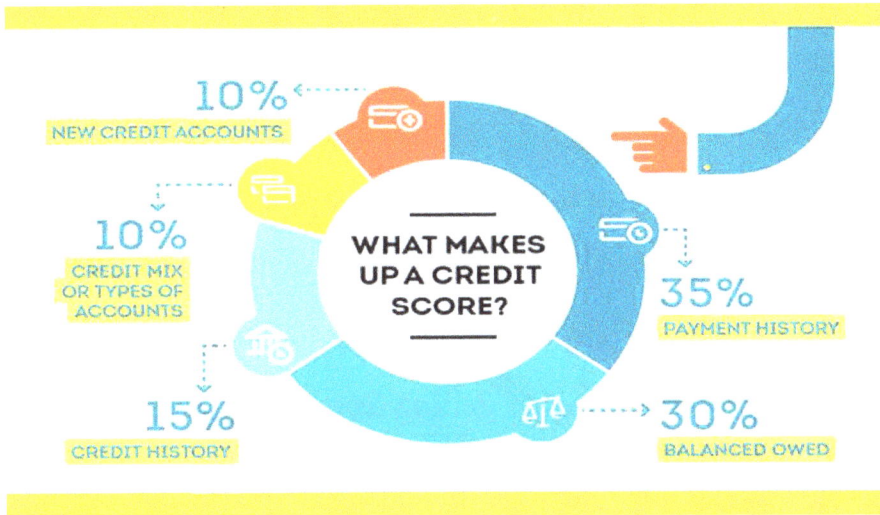

WHAT MAKES UP A CREDIT SCORE?

10% NEW CREDIT ACCOUNTS

10% CREDIT MIX OR TYPES OF ACCOUNTS

15% CREDIT HISTORY

35% PAYMENT HISTORY

30% BALANCED OWED

You'll want to verify there are no errors on the report or recent derogatory items like late payments. Since you may spend months shopping for homes, you might want to consider subscribing to a service that provides regular credit report monitoring for around $20 a month. You can cancel this after you close on your home.

As for your credit score, your estimated FICO credit score should be at least 680 and preferably above 700. Anything less and you may need to find a highly-qualified cosigner or take time to improve your credit before getting mortgage approval. The lower your credit score, the higher the mortgage rate you'll pay.

If your credit is just under 680, you may consider an FHA loan. These government-insured loans allow lower credit scores and much lower down payments, but there are significant additional costs.

Finally, do not apply for new credit in the few months leading up to your mortgage application. Banks get suspicious if it looks like you're piling on the new credit. My mortgage broker once told me that even getting a credit check for a new cell phone plan could require a letter of explanation to your mortgage lender.

3. Determine your mortgage budget

Before ever speaking with a mortgage officer, you'll want to determine how much of a house payment you can afford and are comfortable paying (two different things!).

A good rule is that your total housing payment (including fees, taxes, and insurance) should be no more than 35 percent of your gross (pre-tax) income.

For example, if together you and a co-buyer earn $80,000 a year, your combined maximum housing payment would be $2,333 a month. That's an absolute max, however. I recommend sticking with a total housing payment of 25 percent of your gross income. You'll find other readers here who are even more conservative.

It can be difficult to equate this monthly payment to a fixed home price, as your monthly housing payment is subject to variables like mortgage interest rate, property taxes, the cost of home insurance and private mortgage insurance (PMI), and any condo or association fees.

4. Figure out how much you can save for a down payment

Next, determine how much you can save for a down payment to put towards your first home. In today's market, expect your mortgage lender to require at least a 10 percent down payment unless you're getting an FHA loan or another special program loan.

If you have it, consider putting 20 percent down to avoid private mortgage insurance (PMI). PMI is costly insurance that protects your mortgage lender should you foreclose before building sufficient equity in the property.

Commit to the maximum you want to spend before beginning the mortgage approval process. Real estate agents, your desires, and some unscrupulous mortgage lenders may try to tempt you into buying a more expensive home than you can afford, perhaps rationalizing the decision by reminding you that real estate is bound to appreciate. That may happen, but I would take a smaller payment you can afford in good and bad times over a bigger one that you may lose in a foreclosure.

When and Where to Apply for Your Mortgage

Potential Minimum Down Payment Amount by Mortgage Type & Credit Score		
Mortgage Type	FICO Score	Minimum Down Payment
Conventional	680+	3.0%
Conventional	620-679	5.0%
Conventional - No PMI	620+	20.0%
FHA-Insured	580+	3.5%
FHA-Insured	500-579	10.0%
VA	N/A	No Minimum Required
USDA	N/A	No Minimum Required

You can meet with a mortgage lender and get pre-qualified at any time. Prequalified simply means the lender thinks that, based on your credit score, income, and other factors, you should be able to get approved for a mortgage. It's informal and non-binding.

As you get closer to buying a home, you'll want to seek preapproval. You can meet with a local bank, credit union, or mortgage broker. Or you can even get pre-approved online from any number of national online mortgage lenders.

Wherever you go, this pre-approval isn't binding, but it's a formal(ish) indicator of your ability to get approved for a mortgage. Most sellers will want to see a pre-approval within a couple of days after receiving your offer.

With all the people, paperwork, and time-intensive steps involved, getting a mortgage can seem a little like running an obstacle course. But if you take the time to understand the home buying process and approach it with a strong sense of your own finances, you can hurdle, balance, and sprint your way around the course without a scratch.

Here's how to get a mortgage, step by step (or you can jump to the step you're currently working on):

Step 1: Get your credit in good standing

Step 2: Get preapproved for a mortgage

Step 3: Choose the right mortgage

Step 4: Find the right lender

Step 5: Submit your application

Step 6: Begin the underwriting process

Step 7: Prepare for the closing process

Step 8: Close on the home

1. Get your credit in good standing

Before you set off to get a mortgage, make sure you're financially prepared for homeownership.

➤ Do you have a lot of debt?

➤ Do you have plenty saved for a down payment?

➤ What about closing costs?

Ask yourself, "how much house can I afford?" before you go further.

Additionally, know that lenders look closely at your credit score when determining your eligibility for a mortgage loan. Check your credit score and do anything you can to improve it, such as lowering outstanding debt, disputing any errors, and holding off on applying for any other loans or credit cards. Once you've thoroughly assessed your finances and gotten your credit in tiptop shape, you're ready to research and choose the best mortgage type for you. Below are some options:

o Get your free credit score report. (creditreport.com)

　o Open more doors for your financial goals.

　o Set your goals and see your progress.

　o Signing up won't affect your score.

2. Get preapproved for a mortgage

After you've checked your credit, getting preapproved for a mortgage will tell you how much the lender is comfortable letting you borrow for a home. Once you have your price range, you're ready to look at houses. Getting preapproved also gives you a leg up when you start looking, because it shows sellers that you can make a solid offer up to a specific price.

You don't have to stick with the same lender once you're ready to apply for the loan. But if you do, the process will go a little quicker since you've started the ball rolling with paperwork and a credit check.

3. **Choose the right mortgage**

MORTGAGE LOANS
Which Loan Is Right For You? EXPLAINED!

CONVENTIONAL	FHA	USDA	VA LOAN
95% LOAN-TO-VALUE MORE FINANCING OPTIONS GOOD CREDIT ALL OCCUPANCY TYPES	95.5% LOAN-TO-VALUE LOW PAYMENTS LOW CREDIT SCORE OPTION EASIER TO QUALIFY	ZERO DOWN PAYMENT LOW PAYMENTS GOOD CREDIT LIMITED TO RURAL AREAS	ZERO DOWN PAYMENT LOW PAYMENTS LIMITED TO ELIGIBLE VETERANS NO MORTGAGE INSURANCE
PURCHASE REFINANCE RENOVATE	10, 15, 20 & 30 YEAR FIXED TERMS 5, 7 & 10 YEAR ARMS 1-4 UNITS	PURCHASE REFINANCE RENOVATE	15 & 30 YEAR FIXED RATE 5 YEAR ADJUSTABLE RATES 1-4 UNITS	PURCHASE REFINANCE	30 YEAR FIXED RATE 102.5% LOAN-TO-VALUE 1 UNIT	PURCHASE REFINANCE RENOVATE	15 & 30 YEAR FIXED RATE 5 YEAR ADJUSTABLE RATES 1-4 UNITS

Some mortgage options include:

Conventional or government-backed loan: Government-backed loans, such as Federal Housing Administration loans, can make it easier for you to buy a home if your credit score isn't great or if you don't have money for a big down payment. Conventional loans come from banks, credit unions, or online lenders, and usually require larger down payments than government-backed loans.

Fixed or adjustable-rate: Fixed-rate mortgages tend to be safer because the mortgage interest rate won't change over the life of the loan.

Mortgage term: Do you want a 10-year, 20-year, or 30-year mortgage? With a 30-year term, your monthly payments probably will be smaller, but you'll pay more interest over the life of the loan.

Know your annual percentage rate (APR). This likely will be higher than the quoted interest rate because the APR includes all the associated costs such as origination fees and points. We'll get into points later. Don't borrow more than you can handle.

4. Find the right lender

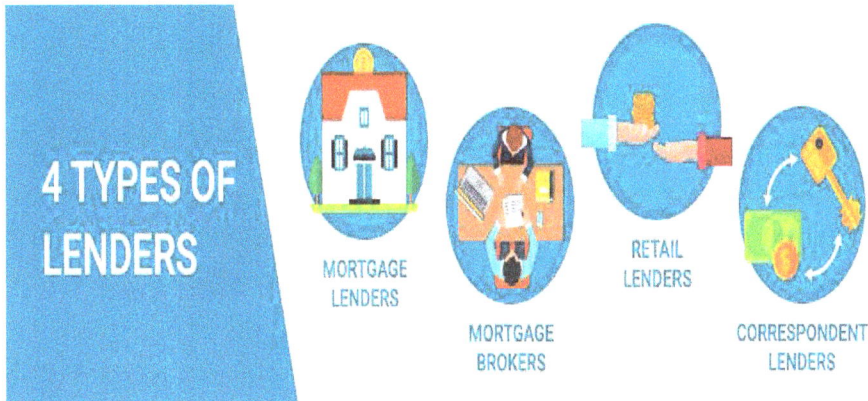

4 TYPES OF LENDERS

MORTGAGE LENDERS

MORTGAGE BROKERS

RETAIL LENDERS

CORRESPONDENT LENDERS

Just like you want to get the home that best suits your needs, you'll want to find a lender that best suits you. If you shopped around before getting preapproved, you're already one step ahead.

- Consider using a broker to help you find a lender
- Talk to your real estate agent
- Ask friends and family for referrals
- Compare at least three lenders. Ask about fees and down payment requirements
- Check current mortgage rates to get the best deal

Not Sure Which Lender is Right for You?

If you're thinking of applying for a mortgage, we can help. Answer just a few questions, and we'll match you with a lender that meets your needs.

- ➤ I care most about...
- ➤ Low down payment
- ➤ Online application
- ➤ Fast close time
- ➤ Low rates
- ➤ Face-to-face service

5. Submit your application

If you're using the same lender that preapproved you, you'll have to submit your most recent financial information. If you're going with a new lender, here's the information you'll need:

- ➤ W-2 forms from the past two years
- ➤ Pay stubs from the past 30 days
- ➤ Federal tax returns from the past two years
- ➤ Proof of other sources of income
- ➤ Recent bank statements
- ➤ Details on long-term debts such as a car or student loans
- ➤ ID and Social Security number

There may be other kinds of documentation required, depending on the type of mortgage you're getting.

If you're self-employed, you'll have to provide extra proof of your financial stability, including having a higher credit score or large cash reserves, and possibly providing business tax returns.

Within three days of receiving your application, your lender will give you a loan estimate which includes:

- How much the loan will cost
- Associated fees and closing costs
- Interest rate, and possibly information on obtaining a rate lock

What's next? Keep an eye on mortgage interest rates. If they start going up, you may want to lock your rate quickly. If they go down, consider waiting.

6. Begin the underwriting process

This part can be the most nerve-wracking, even if you've been preapproved. It's more waiting; this time to get officially approved for the loan.

During the underwriting process, the lender determines whether you're eligible for the loan. Factors evaluated include:

➢ **Credit and job history**
➢ **Debt-to-income ratio**

➢ **Current debt obligations**

The lender then orders a property appraisal and credit report. An appraisal tells the lender the market value of your home, which it matches against the loan amount to see if what you're asking for makes sense.

Meanwhile, you will schedule a home inspection, which will look for any defects in the home. Then you may negotiate repairs or a lower sale price before closing.

During the underwriting process, you'll want to avoid making changes such as switching jobs or taking out another line of credit. Also, avoid large purchases that increase your debt. Increasing your debt can lower your credit score, which could make the loan costlier.

7. Prepare for the closing process

Finally, your loan is approved. But you've got a few more steps to take before the process is complete.

Decide if you should get discount points. Do you want to pay an upfront fee—known as points—to lower your interest rate? This could be a good option if you plan on staying in your home for at least seven years.

Purchase homeowner's insurance. Your lender will require you to do this. Shop around for the best policies. If you don't have insurance by closing, your lender might choose a more expensive policy for you.

Buy a lender's title policy. And while it's not required, it's wise to also purchase owner's title insurance. Both policies protect the lender and you in case there are problems with the title of the property down the road.

Do a final walk-through of the home. Make sure nothing has changed—and the agreed-upon repairs have been made—since the home inspection.

Receive a closing disclosure. You'll get this three days before the scheduled closing date, which lists all the closing costs.

Get a cashier's check. This will be from your bank to cover closing costs.

8. Close on the home

You're almost done! Here's how the last step usually unfolds.

New mortgage closing rules set up by the Consumer Financial Protection Bureau might extend the closing process to simplify all the paperwork before closing and avoiding any surprises.

Typically, you'll pay between 2 percent and 5 percent of the home's purchase price in closing costs. You can estimate your expenses using a closing costs calculator.

You'll also probably have to pay for private mortgage insurance if your down payment is less than 20percent of the home's purchase price. This monthly expense is typical on low-down-payment mortgages to protect lenders in case the borrower fails to repay their loan. Once you get up to 20percent equity in the home, you can take steps to cancel your PMI.

If you start having second thoughts at this point—maybe it's all much more expensive than you thought it would be—you can still walk away. You might lose your deposit, also called earnest money, if you decide not to close. Keep in mind that some fees are negotiable. It's also not unusual for sellers and lenders to pay some of the closing costs.

State laws will determine who is present at closing. These people may include:

> **Your lender**
> **Your real estate agent**
> **A closing agent**

- ➢ **Your attorney**
- ➢ **The seller's attorney**
- ➢ **A title company representative**
- ➢ **The seller and the seller's agent**

Don't be afraid to ask questions. Getting a mortgage comes with a lot of paperwork. Take the time to understand it all. Know what you're signing and what you're paying.

And that's it—you made it through the mortgage obstacle course, and the loan is yours. It's finally time to move into your new home.

Consumer Statements

When Should I Include a Consumer Statement on My Credit Report?

General Consumer Statements
- Identity theft
- Delinquency on multiple accounts as a result of extended unemployment
- Delinquency due to natural or declared disaster
- Financial hardship due to illness or injury

Account Specific Statements
- Response to fraud
- A problem with a lender
- A dispute on your credit report was denied

Source: CreditCardInsider.com

Under the Fair Credit Reporting Act, you are allowed to add a 100-word "consumer statement" to any credit reports if you have disputed an item, but it was not removed due to verification of the debt. At times, consumers think there is an advantage to adding a consumer statement.

Individuals feel it gives them a chance to divulge what happened, elaborate on the dispute, or perhaps explain why going through a divorce resulted in a bad credit issue. Perhaps you may be of the assumption it's better to prove why something was not your fault, or at the very least show the lender you had a good reason for failing to pay the debt.

The Lender's Point of View

The truth, from a lender's standpoint, especially in today's economic environment, there is no single reason under the sun that can justify something negative in your credit report. Creditors want to know whether you paid your debts as agreed, or not. Period. So don't fool yourself into thinking that your consumer statement will be "taken into account."

It won't. In fact, your 100-word statement will most likely be viewed as confirmation that you were financially irresponsible, perhaps because you didn't manage your finances during some unexpected event such as a divorce or a layoff. Nor will it help your cause to have a consumer statement, because it lumps you in the same category as all the other credit damaged individuals who are using consumer statements to plead their case.

My advice about consumer statements is simple: refrain from putting any statement on your credit file. For those of you fretting over something in your credit file, and worried that it may damage your chances of getting a needed loan, fear not. Chances are it will be approved or denied solely based on numbers, not words.

The numbers apply to your **FICO score**, how much debt you are carrying, or financial income. If your application is truly in a gray area and a potential lender has a question, rest assured they'll ask if they need more information to approve your loan. At that point, you can write a letter

directly to that lender, succinctly explaining anything you feel is necessary. You don't need to put explanations in a credit report, because scores of businesses and others will see it, and may even view the consumer statement as an admission of guilt (so to speak), and as proof that you aren't a good credit risk because you couldn't pay your bills on time.

Another practical reason to avoid consumer statements is that they will remain on your credit report for 10 years. Assume you had a dispute with a creditor and, through your perseverance or some settlement, you resolved the matter. The dispute is over. The creditor may even agree to delete negative information, change your payment status, or update the credit history; all of which could wipe away any reference to the matter. But, if you have that consumer statement still lingering on your credit file, it will be a "heads up" to potential lenders and others that—at one point—you were late with a bill or had some dispute with a creditor.

The worst possible issue on credit reports is bad payment history. It is something you should avoid at all costs. If the blemish on your record occurred, say, four years ago, it will come off your credit file in another three years. However, if you added a consumer statement subsequently—perhaps just a year ago—then the statement referencing the black mark will remain another nine years, which is six more years than the late payment itself was shown!

Hopefully, your credit reports currently indicate, "there is no consumer statement associated with this file," or something to that effect. If not, you can dispute an existing consumer statement, or simply write a letter to the credit bureaus and try to get it deleted. For example, TransUnion allows individuals to write a letter to add or remove a consumer statement from their credit reports.

To get a consumer statement removed, send a consumer statement removal request, along with your name, address, and TransUnion File Identification Number to:

TransUnion Consumer Relations
P.O. Box 2000
Chester, PA 19022

If you write the credit agencies to delete a consumer statement and it doesn't work, just be prepared to wait it out until any consumer statement you supplied to the credit bureaus eventually expires.

Chapter Three:

Banking

Your credit score is more than just a three-digit number. It's an important financial tool that lenders use to determine how responsible you are when it comes to managing your money. Several things affect your credit score, including your payment history and the amount of debt you have. But your banking habits can also make a difference. While swiping your debit card or writing a check won't affect your score directly, how you handle your bank account can impact your creditworthiness.

CREDIT UNIONS VS. BANKS: WHAT'S THE DIFFERENCE?

Pros and Cons of Banks	Pros and Cons of Credit Unions
• Interest rates: vary depending on the size of the bank, but interest rates are generally lower than credit unions	• Interest rates: in most cases, interest rates are higher than banks
• Fees: typically higher than most credit unions	• Fees: typically lower than most banks
• Best for: convenience	• Best for: high interest rates, strong customer service, and good loans

Do Checking Accounts Affect Your Credit Score?

Your traditional credit report only tracks your credit and debt situation. If you have a checking or savings account at a bank, credit union, or brokerage firm, the following transactions will not appear on a credit report or credit score:

> ➢ **Making a deposit or withdrawal**
> ➢ **Writing a check**
> ➢ **Closing an account**
> ➢ **Having multiple accounts**

If you have a check overdraft, it still will not appear on your report unless you do not pay the fees and the bank turns the bill over to a collection agency.

There are a few instances where a checking account could affect your traditional credit score. Some banks or credit unions may look at your credit report when you open a new account. They will usually do a "soft pull," meaning they check your credit, but it does not affect your credit score. Some banks may do a "hard pull" or "hard inquiry," though usually those are only used by lenders when you are requesting the credit or a loan. If the bank does a hard pull, it will impact your credit score for up to 12 months, usually by dropping your score by five points or fewer.

The second way a checking account may affect your credit score is if you sign up for overdraft protection on the account. Doing so sets up a new line of credit, possibly triggering a credit report inquiry and a report from the bank to the three major credit reporting bureaus. But this is not always the case—not all overdraft accounts are reported. To find out if your account may be reported, ask your bank directly.

Even if a bank doesn't report a new checking account to the credit bureaus, it may check with ChexSystems, a consumer reporting agency for financial institutions. Banks's report mishandled checking and savings accounts to ChexSystems, which in turn shares that information back to banks to help determine the risk of opening new accounts. Reports to ChexSystems stay on file for five years.

Opening New Accounts

When opening a new checking or savings account, the bank may decide to do a quick credit check before you're approved. The bank has the option of doing a hard or soft pull. A soft inquiry generally doesn't affect your score but a hard inquiry will show up on your credit history.

The number of inquiries you have makes up 10percent of your FICO® score and each inquiry can reduce your score by 5 to 10 points. If you're trying to open multiple credit cards, loans, or bank accounts over a relatively short period it could add up to a significant drop. If you're planning to open a new account, check with the bank first to see what kind of inquiry is required.

Closing an Account

When it comes to your credit, the age of your accounts is a major factor in determining your score. The longer a credit card or line of credit has been open, the better. Therefore, closing older credit card accounts can work against you. When you close a checking account, age isn't a factor but it's still possible that it could affect your score.

If you're closing an account with an outstanding overdraft or the bank closes your account because it suspects fraud or other criminal activity, it could show up on your credit. Whether the information is reported through ChexSystems or the three major credit reporting bureaus is ultimately up to the bank. If, however, you're closing an account because you've found a better deal somewhere else your bank can't hold this against you.

Banks are responsible for reporting negative information to ChexSystems and it can remain on your credit history for up to five years. Some of the reasons you may be reported include frequent bounced checks, excessive overdraft fees, or abandoning an account with a negative balance. If you write a check to a business that uses ChexSystems, the transaction may be denied based on the information in your file.

What's in your credit report can have a major impact on your finances in terms of whether you're able to get approved for new credit and the amount of interest you'll pay. Managing all your accounts responsibly, including your bank account, is one of the easiest ways to maintain a healthy score.

Overdrafts and Your Credit Score

Alternatives to Overdraft Protection

- Signing up for email or text alerts
- Using a transfer service
- Monitoring your online banking account
- Downloading a mobile banking app
- Using your credit card for purchases

Overdraft simply means that you've spent more money than you had in your account. Typically, the bank covers the difference and charges you a fee for doing so. Overdrafts can occur for several reasons. Maybe you wrote a check and forgot about it or a deposit didn't clear right away. When it only happens once, an overdraft usually isn't that big of a deal.

If, however, you've racked up a significant amount of overdraft and you don't have enough cash to bring your account out of the red it can mean trouble where your credits concerned. Eventually, the bank may decide to close your account and refer the debt to a collection agency. At this point, you'll likely receive a black mark on your credit that can stay in place for up to seven years.

Virtually all banks now offer some form of overdraft protection; although, you may have to specifically request this service. Depending on the bank, you may be charged a separate service fee if you decide to opt-in. Certain banks offer overdraft protection that's reported as a revolving account or line of credit. Credit reporting bureaus view this type of overdraft as being equal to a credit card when calculating your score. If you routinely keep a low balance in your checking account, signing up for overdraft protection may be worth it to keep your credit intact.

Bouncing Checks

It used to be that if you wrote a check, it would take a week or more to clear. Nowadays, checks can clear in a matter of one or two days which makes it vital that you have enough money in your account to cover them. To cut down on the number of bad checks they receive, many businesses choose to use ChexSystems.

Fintech Companies vs. Traditional Banks

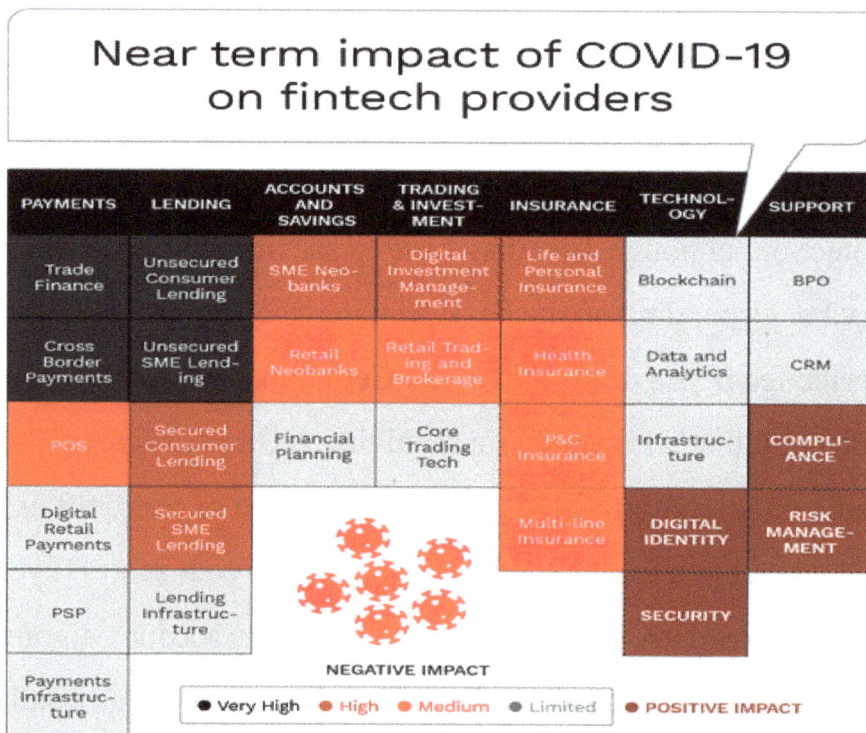

Near term impact of COVID-19 on fintech providers

PAYMENTS	LENDING	ACCOUNTS AND SAVINGS	TRADING & INVEST-MENT	INSURANCE	TECHNOL-OGY	SUPPORT
Trade Finance	Unsecured Consumer Lending	SME Neo-banks	Digital Investment Manage-ment	Life and Personal Insurance	Blockchain	BPO
Cross Border Payments	Unsecured SME Lend-ing	Retail Neobanks	Retail Trad-ing and Brokerage	Health Insurance	Data and Analytics	CRM
POS	Secured Consumer Lending	Financial Planning	Core Trading Tech	P&C Insurance	Infrastruc-ture	COMPLI-ANCE
Digital Retail Payments	Secured SME Lending			Multi-line Insurance	DIGITAL IDENTITY	RISK MANAGE-MENT
PSP	Lending Infrastruc-ture				SECURITY	
Payments Infrastruc-ture						

NEGATIVE IMPACT

● Very High   ● High   ● Medium   ● Limited   ● POSITIVE IMPACT

Traditional banks are simplifying their organizational structure to reduce overhead costs and are focusing on their core competencies rather than trying to excel at everything, according to a report by Deloitte. With the rise of the fintech industry, startups, and online banking companies looking to exploit the weaknesses of large financial institutions, the banking landscape must keep up with the changing times.

But newer, progressive options don't necessarily mean that traditional banks are a poor choice—it just depends on each customer's particular needs. Banks are adding electronic banking, mobile check deposit, and alerts to their services while continuing to provide the traditional services most customers are used to—in-person assistance, mortgage loans, and more. And as traditional banks up their game to compete with the more flexible online alternatives, consumers can benefit from these changes. Learn about the advantages and disadvantages of banks so you can decide what kind of financial institution is best for your money.

Pros of Traditional Banks

Although using a traditional bank might seem old-school or too conventional, there are certain benefits of banking with a financial institution that has brick-and-mortar branches. Knowing some of the banking benefits of using a traditional institution can help you decide if it's a good solution for keeping and handling your money.

1. More Options

Whether you want personal savings or checking account, trust fund, certificate of deposit, Roth IRA, or business checking account, most major financial institutions can provide all these services in one place. Many traditional banks also offer wealth management and investment services.

2. Convenience

The leading banks—Chase, Wells Fargo, and Bank of America—have brick-and-mortar locations and ATMs all over the country that are free to customers.,

3. Best of Both Worlds

Many banks offer customers the flexibility of being able to walk into a branch to deposit cash or to transfer money via a smartphone. Chase Bank, for example, offers QuickPay—a free online service to send or receive money by email— which competes with fintech apps like Venmo and Square Cash. With online banks, you only have the electronic transfer option.

4. Cash Deposits

Despite all the progress that fintech has made, the industry still has to contend with a traditional form of currency: cash. For banking customers who deal with cash frequently, a traditional bank is an attractive and convenient option.

Cons of Traditional Banks

Banks can offer critical conveniences but are not without their flaws. To help you decide if a traditional bank is a right solution for your financial needs, here are some of the drawbacks to banking at a larger institution.

1. Low or No Interest Rates

Brick-and-mortar banks are notorious for their lower interest rates on savings accounts compared with online banks. In fact, in a recent survey by GOBankingRates, many of the best savings' accounts were with online banks: Synchrony Bank, Ally Bank, and iGObanking.com offered some of the highest interest rates.

2. Wide Range of Fees

When you think of a traditional bank, you might also think of bank fees. Bank of America, for example, charges a $35 nonsufficient funds fee, whereas Alliant Credit Union— one of the largest credit unions open to the public—charges just $25 for an NSF fee.

A study by Consumer Reports suggested that one of the major downfalls of big banks is that they don't understand customers' needs and don't provide personalized service. According to the survey, the four megabanks—Bank of America, Chase, Citibank, and Wells Fargo—which hold approximately 40 percent of all U.S. commercial bank assets, landed in the bottom fifth of the customer satisfaction rankings. Smaller financial institutions have a smaller demographic, but this seems to help them gain insight into who's banking with them and what those customers want.

Alternatives to Large Banks

When deciding where to put your money, there are many options to consider, including credit unions, online banks, and local brick-and-mortar banks. Each of these alternatives to megabanks offers advantages, depending on your needs.

Credit unions: Credit unions are financial institutions that are cooperatively owned by all members and democratically run by members who volunteer as board members. The members vote on issues like interest rates, and because these institutions are not for profit, account holders usually get better rates on both loans and savings interest. Credit unions are insured by the National Credit Union Administration, so a member's money is secure.

Online banks: Serving as another alternative to traditional banks, online banks such as Ally Bank, Simple, or Bank 5 Connect tend to offer more favorable services and rates. For example, Ally Bank offers up to 0.60% APY on its checking accounts whereas Bank of America offers a maximum of just 0.02% APY. Online banks don't have to spend money on supporting many physical locations, so they're able to pass on these savings to customers.

Community and local banks: Community banks are a vital part of many areas, especially rural and farming communities, which depend on local banks for loans and basic services. Because these areas are usually tight-knit, these types of banks are more flexible with loan requirements than big banks. For example, the Independent Community Bankers of America Association says it considers character, family history, and discretionary spending in making loans; this is not the kind of service you could typically expect to find in a big, traditional bank.

No Matter What You Choose, Safety Rules

Regardless of your choice in banking, the FDIC recommends that consumers verify the legitimacy of the bank and that all deposits are federally insured. The FDIC has a database of all insured banks that the public can access, so you can easily confirm if your bank is covered. And whether you choose a traditional bank with online banking features or an online-only bank, be aware of copycat websites that deliberately use a web address similar to that of a real bank to lure in unsuspecting customers.

Chapter Four:

Budgeting

Life was easy when your only obligations were a portion of the rent, cable, and utility bills with an occasional trip to the grocery. Nevertheless, adulthood beckoned, and it's time to create a budget and pay bills on time, every time. Now that you're either a homeowner or saving for your first home, sticking to a budget and paying bills is important to your financial well-being. Creating a budget will curb your spending and help launch a savings plan that will lead you down the path to financial stability.

Tip:

Check your bank accounts online often so you always know how much money is in your account.

Warnings:

> ➤ Paying bills on time will avoid late fees and increased charges
> ➤ Leave credit cards at home so you are not tempted
> ➤ Don't stray from your budget. Be honest with your life partner or family members who help pay the bills

It takes commitment and time, but anyone can learn to manage money even with a minimal income. A real-world budget often doesn't apply when you're struggling to make ends meet. However, the basic concepts are the same, but your breakdown of spending will probably be different. Everyone's situation is unique. Below are some essential guidelines to follow.

1. Assess Your Financial Situation

If you have more money going out than coming in, here's what your financial plan boils down to spend less and/or earn more.

To figure out how to do this, first take an assessment of your income and expenses. This will help you develop a realistic budget.

2. Categorize Your Expenses

Break down your expenses over the past few months. Categorize them into needs and wants. Separating will help you prioritize your finances. To get a clear idea of your needs and wants, consider creating a hierarchy of spending. Organize your debts.

3. Identify Your Problem Spending Areas

Take note of your spending habits. Are there any specific stores you frequent? Do you have a coffee habit that can be cut? Many times, there are "leaks" in a budget that can be plugged. The first step is figuring out where they are. Identify these categories and keep them in mind once you start your budget.

4. Cut Back Your Spending

Find ways to reduce your expenses. The first place to start is the "wants" category. It's important to allow yourself a little breathing room for fun in your budget. If you don't, you risk faulting, and that can make you want to quit altogether. But remember, the key to managing your money when you're broke is downsizing your lifestyle. If you can't afford to pay your bills, take a close look at what might be luxuries. Here are some examples of unnecessary expenses:

Once the wants are out of the way, take a look at your needs. You may find large savings, particularly on your bills. Many times, you can change a service provider, cut electric bills by adjusting your thermostat, or change phone companies, television services, etc.

5. Be Frugal

When you're struggling to make ends meet, frugality is your friend. Make the most out of your money and the things you spend it on. For example, you could:

➢ Stretch your meals

➢ Cut down on extras at the store

➢ Consider a diet change

Do It Yourself: One of the best ways to cut costs is to learn to do things yourself rather than pay for them. For example, you can save some money by learning basic preventive car maintenance, taking on home projects, and making your cleaning products and toiletries.

Save on Housing: Can you negotiate your rent? Can you move to a cheaper place? Since this is likely one of your biggest expenses, it's one of the best ways to make a dent in your spending.

Your options will vary. The point is to adopt a frugal lifestyle and look for opportunities to trim costs. Once you have established your budget and gain some headway, then you can treat yourself and your family later. Plan activities based on your income.

6. Prioritize Your Money Goals

Many people wonder whether they should focus on debt or savings first. The answer depends on your situation. But, if your debt is extensive, cutting the cost of paying obligations can increase your income. This will allow you to put money aside for emergencies.

Setbacks are inevitable. If you're not prepared for them, they can devastate your budget and your finances. While it might take some time to build an emergency fund, it will allow you to stick to your budget if a financial setback arises.

7. Tackle Your Debt

Whatever you choose to focus on, don't risk your finances unraveling by ignoring your debt. Late fees and interest can turn a small debt into an overwhelming one. Your debt should be a priority.

8. Pick a Repayment Method

You'll have to come up with a debt repayment plan. To do this; first, pick a method:

A. Pay your smallest debts to build self-motivation. Seeing your financial freedom increase quickly will improve your determination to continue.

B. Pay debts with the highest interest first to lower the risk of additional costs. The expense of increased interest rates and late fees can amplify quickly.

9. Reduce Your Credit Card Interest Rate

Yes, it's possible. According to Bankrate, a national survey found that 56 percent of consumers who called credit card companies to ask for a lower interest rate had positive results.

10. Request Extensions or Payment Plans

Don't be afraid to request bill extensions or payment plans. These requests are often granted. If your biggest worry is eviction from your apartment, talk to your landlord, but also see if you can get extensions on any other expenses to free up money to keep your home.

Playing catch-up might derail you from your other financial goals. But the most important thing is to keep your debts organized and come up with a plan on how to tackle each one.

Draft Your Plan

Every cent will be accounted for, making your budget tight. At this point, a traditional budget strategy may not be suited for you. But don't risk blowing your budget either. Avoid the following mistakes:

Not being realistic: Crunch the numbers realistically. Set a reasonable amount aside for each of your expenses. Maybe your plan to eat for $25 a month is too extreme. It's probably not going to work. Don't set yourself up for failure.

Cutting out all the fun: It's important to give yourself some breathing room. Limit yourself without leaving you deprived. The outcome may cause overspending.

The amount of breathing room will depend on your situation. But it should only be enough to keep you from blowing your budget. Set aside an appropriate, but modest amount.

Brainstorm your plan of attack. Once you pick your debt repayment strategy, allocate an amount toward each debt. Calculate how long it will take to eliminate each one with your budget in place. Breaking up goals into smaller milestones makes them easier to achieve.

Take Advantage of Opportunities: Part of managing money when broke is increasing your income. For example, you might be able to:

> ➤ Get a better job
> ➤ Ask for a raise
> ➤ Sell your stuff
> ➤ Find a side gig

Some options may not be available to everyone, but the point is to find what works for you and your family then stick to the plan. It's ultimately about being resourceful. Look for opportunities to earn and save more money, then take advantage of those situations. It may seem like a sacrifice, but keep your eye on the end game.

Personal Monthly Budget

PROJECTED MONTHLY INCOME	Income 1	$2,500
	Extra income	$500
	Total monthly income	$3,000
ACTUAL MONTHLY INCOME	Income 1	$2,500
	Extra income	$500
	Total monthly income	$3,000

TOTAL PROJECTED EXPENSE	(Projected income minus expenses)	$2,060
TOTAL ACTUAL EXPENSE	(Actual income minus expenses)	$2,040
	Total Expense Difference	$20
PROJECTED BALANCE	(Projected income minus expenses)	$940
ACTUAL BALANCE	(Actual income minus expenses)	$960
	BALANCE DIFFERENCE (Actual minus projected)	$20

HOUSING	Projected Cost	Actual Cost	Difference
Mortgage or rent	$1,500	$1,400	$100
Phone	$60	$100	-$40
Electricity	$50	$60	-$10
Gas	$200	$180	$20
Water and sewer			$0
Cable			$0
Waste removal			$0
Maintenance or repairs			$0
Supplies			$0
Other			$0
Total	$1,810	$1,740	$70

TRANSPORTATION	Projected Cost	Actual Cost	Difference
Vehicle payment	$250	$250	$0
Bus/taxi fare			$0
Insurance			$0
Licensing			$0
Fuel			$0
Maintenance			$0
Other			$0
Total	$250	$250	$0

INSURANCE	Projected Cost	Actual Cost	Difference
Home			$0
Health			$0
Life			$0
Other			$0
Total	$0	$0	$0

FOOD	Projected Cost	Actual Cost	Difference
Groceries			$0
Dining out			$0
Other			$0
Total	$0	$0	$0

PETS	Projected Cost	Actual Cost	Difference
Food			$0
Medical			$0
Grooming			$0
Toys			$0
Other			$0
Total	$0	$0	$0

PERSONAL CARE	Projected Cost	Actual Cost	Difference
Medical			$0
Hair/nails			$0
Clothing			$0
Dry cleaning			$0
Health club			$0
Organization dues or fees			$0
Other			$0
Total	$0	$0	$0

ENTERTAINMENT	Projected Cost	Actual Cost	Difference
Video/DVD	$0	$50	-$50
CDs			$0
Movies			$0
Concerts			$0
Sporting events			$0
Live theater			$0
Other			$0
Other			$0
Other			$0
Total	$0	$50	-$50

LOANS	Projected Cost	Actual Cost	Difference
Personal			$0
Student			$0
Credit card			$0
Credit card			$0
Credit card			$0
Other			$0
Total	$0	$0	$0

TAXES	Projected Cost	Actual Cost	Difference
Federal			$0
State			$0
Local			$0
Other			$0
Total	$0	$0	$0

SAVINGS OR INVESTMENTS	Projected Cost	Actual Cost	Difference
Retirement account			$0
Investment account			$0
Other			$0
Total	$0	$0	$0

GIFTS AND DONATIONS	Projected Cost	Actual Cost	Difference
Charity 1			$0
Charity 2			$0
Charity 3			$0
Total	$0	$0	$0

LEGAL	Projected Cost	Actual Cost	Difference
Attorney			$0
Alimony			$0
Payments on lien or judgment			$0
Other			$0
Total	$0	$0	$0

Chapter Five:

Statistics

Americans' total credit card debt continued to climb in 2020, reaching an estimated $931 billion—a nearly 7% increase from 2016. The average household that's carrying credit card debt has a balance of $15,983. Households with any kind of debt owe $133,568 (including mortgages) on average, according to the data analysis found.

A 2020 household debt study showed that several major spending categories have outpaced income growth over the past decade. Many Americans are putting medical expenses on credit cards, and the average indebted household is paying hundreds of dollars in credit card interest each year.

It's not all bad news, though. Household income growth is no longer being outpaced by the total cost of living. According to the results of a new survey, a significant number of people with credit card debt blame it on unnecessary spending, which means consumers can choose to cut their spending and pay down their balances. But, before Americans can begin working to lower their debt, it's important to know what the debt balance is. Here's what the typical indebted household owes, as well as total consumer debt balances in the U.S., according to recent polls.

Debit balances are current as of December 2020

Credit Card Debt Drops Sharply as Consumers Cut Back

Quarterly change in total outstanding credit card debt in the United States

Q2 '20 -$76b

The $931 billion in total credit card debt calculated is lower than the $1 trillion commonly cited elsewhere in the media. That's because the $1 trillion estimate includes what's called "prearranged overdraft plans" or overdraft lines of credit that don't necessarily belong to credit card users. With these overdraft plans, consumers can withdraw money and make payments from the account with the credit line up to the credit limit.

Since the focus is on credit card debt only, the $931 billion is a more accurate estimate of how much debt is outstanding. It's also important to note that this total includes the balances of cardholders who pay off their cards in full every month, as well as those who carry debt from one month to the next.

To determine how much debt Americans are carrying and how much it was costing them in 2020, the data was analyzed from several sources, including the Federal Reserve Bank of New York and the U.S. Census Bureau. For this study, NerdWallet used an estimate of more than 126 million U.S. households based on December 2020 Census Bureau data.

A commissioned survey, conducted online by Harris Poll, of more than 2,000 U.S. adults in November 2021 asked Americans about their credit card payment habits and how they got into debt.

Key Findings

Costs have risen, and income hasn't kept up. Over the past decade, medical costs have increased 34percent and food prices went up 22percent, which outpaced income growth (20 percent).

Health care takes a toll. Up to 27 million American adults are putting medical expenses on credit cards, costing them an average of $471 in interest for a year's worth of out-of-pocket medical spending. That's more than $12 billion total.

Credit card debt comes with a cost. The average household with revolving credit card debt pays $904 in interest annually.

Income Grows Faster Than Cost of Living

The median annual household income has grown 20 percent over the past decade, while the cost of living has increased by 18 percent. However, significant expenses in Americans' budgets—medical care, housing, and food—have outpaced income growth.

Four major spending categories have increased faster than income growth since 2007: medical expenses (34%), "other" expenses (30%), food and beverages (22%), and housing (20%).

These expenses are some of the biggest for many Americans. Then add in the higher cost of living in some places or chronic health problems, and it can be even harder for people to live without going into debt.

When it comes to credit card debt, some people think it's the result of overspending, while others blame it on the rising cost of living for necessities. Our survey found that consumers accumulate credit card debt for different reasons, including spending above their means, bouts of unemployment, and paying for the essentials that their income doesn't cover.

About 2 in 5 Americans who have ever had credit card debt (41%) reported that spending more than they could afford on unnecessary purchases contributed to them going into credit card debt. A third (33%) said that spending on necessities their income couldn't cover contributed to their credit card debt balances. The rising cost of living may be partly to blame, particularly in the spending categories, such as health care, that has increased the most over the past decade.

What Can You Do?

The cost of debt includes the opportunities you must forgo in order to pay it off. In the survey, many Americans who have been in credit card debt said that if they didn't have credit card debt to pay off, they would save that money for emergencies (57%), save it for a future goal (50%), and/or put the money toward paying down other debt (33%).

The quickest way to get rid of your debt and start working toward other financial goals is to cut expenses to free up cash for larger debt payments.

Medical Expenses and the Cost of Interest

In the past decade, medical costs have increased 34 percent, which is more than any other major spending category and significantly more than income.

According to a 2016-17 survey by the Kaiser Family Foundation, which focused on the nation's health policies and medical issues, 29 percent of Americans report problems paying medical bills, and 37 percent have increased their credit card debt to help pay for medical bills. Based on the number of adults in the U.S.—almost 250 million as of July 2016—calculations found that nearly 27 million Americans could be putting medical bills on credit cards.

Let's consider what that costs. The average annual out-of-pocket medical spending per capita in the U.S. was $1,054 as of 2015, the most recent data available from Peterson-Kaiser, a partnership between the Peterson Center on Healthcare and the Kaiser Family Foundation. If this amount went on a credit card and minimum payments were made each month, it would cost $471 in interest and take 70 months to pay off.

If all 27 million Americans who put medical bills on a credit card paid this much interest, that would be over $12 billion in total.

Charging medical bills to credit cards can seem like a simple solution, but it can lead to even bigger headaches down the road.

Another way to save money on health care costs is by using a flexible spending arrangement or health savings account offered by your employer. These are tax-free accounts where you set money aside to pay for medical expenses. HSAs are available to people who use a high-deductible health plan, while FSAs don't have eligibility requirements. Putting money in one of these accounts means you'll save on taxes and have cash on hand for medical bills.

Costs of Rising Credit Card Debt

Credit card balances carried from one month to the next hit $413.7 billion in mid-2020, according to NerdWallet's annual analysis of U.S. household debt. Credit card debt has decreased more than 5 percent in the past year but increased by 20 percent in the past five years.

There are two main types of credit card users: transactors, and revolvers. Transactors pay their credit card balances in full every month and don't pay interest. Revolvers carry credit card debt from one month to the next, paying interest on their average daily balance.

In the survey by Nerd Wallet, 61 percent of Americans who have ever owned a credit card said they have carried a balance from one month to the next, either currently or previously.

Credit cards typically have double-digit interest rates, even for consumers with excellent credit, so being a revolver can be expensive. The average U.S. household with revolving credit card debt carried a balance of $6,081 as of June 2021. Assuming an interest rate of 14.87 percent—the current average—that balance would incur $904 in interest per year.

The Price of Self-Employment

Being self-employed has its benefits—flexible work hours, no boss, and the freedom to work on the things that excite you. However, it can also be costly. Irregular income and business expenses could help explain why self-employed individuals have more credit card debt, which leads to higher interest rate costs.

According to DebtWAve, "U.S. households led by self-employed individuals pay $1,194 in credit card interest each year, compared with $843 for those who work for someone else. People who are retired pay an annual average of $684 in credit card interest."

Costs of Homeownership

Some people say renters are throwing away money on rent, but it's clear that they're throwing away less on credit card interest than their home-owning friends. Renters pay just over half of what homeowners do each year.

U.S. Household and Credit Card Debt, 2013-2021

Year	Average credit card debt per household	Average credit card debt per indebted household	Average total debt per household	Average total debt per indebted household
2013	$6,224.53	$16,318.85	$94,080.47	$126,207.12

Year	Average credit card debt per household	Average credit card debt per indebted household	Average total debt per household	Average total debt per indebted household
2014	$6,360.11	$15,875.61	$102,335.89	$135,730.60
2015	$6,587.77	$15,692.23	$103,837.08	$136,183.05
2016	$6,940.53	$15,809.85	$99,953.11	$129,640.87

Year	Average credit card debt per household	Average credit card debt per indebted household	Average total debt per household	Average total debt per indebted household
2021	$7,377.76	$15,982.94	$104,164.03	$133,568.17

Chapter Six:

Credit Bureaus

Credit reporting agencies (CRAs), also known as credit bureaus, gather your credit information to be used when you are applying for loans, credit cards, etc.

Consumer credit history, scores, and reports are extremely important, so we want to make sure you have the facts straight.

Lenders go to the three main credit bureaus— Experian, TransUnion, and Equifax—when looking to pull and review your credit reports. Other CRAs exist but these are the top choices.

There's a lot of confusion when it comes to what the major credit bureaus do. What kind of information do they collect? Where does that information end up? Do they create credit scores or credit reports? And what's the difference? Let's break it down.

What Do the Major Credit Reporting Agencies Do?

EQUIFAX

Products   Customer Service   Finance Blog   Member Center

Equifax 3-in-1 Monitoring with Credit Scores   ▽ Member Services

Credit Watch | Fraud Alert | Score Watch | Credit Report | Credit Score | Debt Wise | Identity Report

» Alerts

» Reports

Credit Score

Summary

Understanding Your Score

Your Loan Risk Rating

Interactive Score Estimator

⊟Credit Report

  Credit Summary

  ⊞Accounts

  Inquiries

  ⊞Negative Information

  Personal Information

  Dispute File Information

Archive

» Insurance

Equifax Credit Report ™   🖨 Print Report

As of: 9/27/2010
Available until: 10/27/2011 – Report Does Not Update   Correct errors in your Credit Report
Confirmation #: 0800859542   Initiate Online Dispute ▶

Credit Summary

Your Equifax Credit Summary highlights the information in your credit file that is most important in determining your credit standing by distilling key credit information into one easy-to-read summary.

Accounts

Lenders usually take a positive view of individuals with a range of credit accounts - car loan, credit cards, mortgage, etc. - that have a record of timely payments. However, a high debt to credit ratio on certain types of revolving (credit card) accounts and installment loans will typically have a negative impact.

Open Accounts	Total Number	Balance	Available ❓	Credit Limit ❓	Debt to Credit Ratio	Monthly Payment Amount ❓	Accounts with a Balance
Mortgage	1	$2,241	$0	$5,000	45%	$0	1
Installment	0	$0	N/A	N/A	N/A	$0	0
Revolving	1	$1,500	-$1500	$0	0%	$0	1
Other	0	$0	N/A	N/A	N/A	$0	0
Total	2	$3,741	-$1,500	$5,000	75%	$0	2

The short answer is that the credit reporting agencies compile details about your credit history so potential lenders can see what type of risk they'd be taking in giving you a new credit card or loan.

The major credit bureaus are all for-profit companies and are not owned by the government. They have reporting relationships with banks, credit card issuers, lenders, and other financial organizations and compile your credit history into credit reports.

To contact any credit bureau directly on the phone, check their individual websites for more information.

Why Do We Really Have Credit Bureaus?

Credit bureaus are in place to help consumers and business owners alike with the vetting process. Before we had the three credit reporting agencies in place, people would loan money on their own accord without having the convenience of being able to check the individual's payment history or anything. Loans were given solely based on trustworthiness.

However, cities began to grow, and more and more people began to need credit and loans, and this made it more difficult for a lender to know who was going to be able to pay their bills or not if they did business with them. Therefore, enter the three major credit bureaus.

What Kind of Information Do Credit Bureaus Collect?

Credit reports include information about your existing credit accounts as well as your payment history from a variety of financial institutions, including credit card companies, banks, mortgage companies, and other lenders you may have worked with in the past.

Other businesses, such as telephone and utility companies, may also report information to the credit reporting agencies. However, non-lending organizations like these tend to only report delinquent payments and other negative information (an account sent to collections, for example).

The major credit reporting agencies collect a lot of information, but there are five key factors listed on your credit reports that are generally used to determine your creditworthiness when you need a loan or additional line of credit.

These factors are your payment history, the types of accounts in your credit file, your amount of debt, how long you've had credit, and the number of hard inquiries that appear on your credit file.

What Is Done with This Information?

Once the major credit reporting agencies have collected all the information, compiled your credit history, and generated a credit report, they sell that information back to the lenders, so they can determine your creditworthiness.

Based on your credit report and credit score, lenders can decide whether or not to lend you money. If they decide you're someone they want to do business with, the information supplied by the credit bureaus will be used to help determine what your interest rate will be.

How Long Do Credit Bureaus Keep My Information?

Personal information (your name, address, etc.) as well as positive financial information (a strong payment history) can remain on your credit reports indefinitely.

The credit bureaus compile more troubling information as well to give insight on how risky of a potential borrower you are. Most of these details can remain on your credit reports for seven years, but the timeline can vary depending on the item.

Here's a breakdown of how long some of the negative information collected by the credit bureaus will likely stay on your credit reports.

- ➢ **Bankruptcy:** Ten years from the date of filing for Chapter 7 filings, seven years for Chapter 13 filings, and seven years for each record marked as "Included in BK"
- ➢ **Charge-Offs:** (when a creditor or lender writes off the balance of delinquent debt and no longer expects it to be repaid) Seven years
- ➢ **Closed Accounts:** Seven years if the account was paid late; no expiration date if the account was always paid on time
- ➢ **Collection Accounts:** Seven years from the last late payment on the original account

- ➤ **Inquiries:** Two years
- ➤ **Late Payments:** Seven years from the date of the late payment
- ➤ **Judgments:** Seven years from the filing date if paid; longer if unpaid
- ➤ **Tax Liens:** Seven years from the date the lien is paid, and could remain indefinitely if left unpaid

Do All Three Credit Bureaus Have the Same Information?

The three main credit bureaus all operate independently of each other, so they don't share information or communicate at all. Thus, your credit file from each bureau may be slightly different.

It's a good idea to review each of your reports from the three big credit bureaus (Experian, TransUnion, and Equifax), so you can verify that everything on each credit report is accurate.

If you find something is inaccurate on any of your reports, you'll want to dispute it, which you can do on your own or get help from a credit repair expert, Dr. Credit King.

It's important to note that if an error appears on multiple reports, you'll need to file a separate dispute with each credit bureau reporting the misinformation. You can file disputes with each of the major credit reporting agencies via their websites or by mail.

How Do You Get a Copy of Your Credit Reports?

Federal law entitles you to one free credit report from each bureau every twelve months. You can request your free annual credit reports from Equifax, Experian, and TransUnion at AnnualCreditReport.com. If you need to get an additional credit report during the year, you can purchase one directly from each of the major credit bureaus.

Equifax and Experian have available credit files that include all three main credit reports on a single page.

By reviewing your report, you'll get insight into how you're doing in the five-credit report focus areas we mentioned earlier. You'll also see two of your credit scores for free.

A personalized step-by-step action plan is also available, so you know where to focus your credit-improving efforts to achieve your goals.

Understanding the Difference Between Credit Reports and Credit Scores

Credit Report vs. Credit Score: What's the Difference?

A credit report shows your borrowing history; this information is then used to **generate your credit score.**

CREDIT SCORE

Your credit score is a **numerical grade of your creditworthiness** at any given time.

700

620

720

CREDIT REPORT

Your credit report lists every piece of your financial history that **affects your creditworthiness.**

Number/type of accounts
Credit age
Late payment history
Credit utilization rate
Number of hard inquiries
Overall debt amount

Now that you have a bit more insight into what information the credit bureaus collect and how they use this information, you may be wondering what the difference is between the credit reports they issue and the credit scores you hear so much about.

Basically, the information in your credit reports is used to generate your three-digit credit score, which is a numerical representation of your creditworthiness.

Because there are three major credit reporting agencies, and the information collected by them can vary, your credit scores may also vary depending on what credit bureau a lender is using to ascertain your credit history.

Beyond that, there are many different credit scoring models or formulas, which change from lender to lender. In fact, you've probably heard of a FICO score before. But you don't have just one FICO score, you have dozens.

Experian Credit Reports

You can find your Experian credit report on AnnualCreditReport.com and can access it for free once per year. Once you receive the copy of your credit report, check the entire report for accuracy and make note of any discrepancies there may be, so you can submit a dispute to the reporting agency to potentially have them removed.

To file a dispute with Experian, you can do it online by following their instructions on the site, or you can send in the proper documentation and evidence by mail, so they can review everything and investigate the dispute.

The Experian credit score is a FICO 8 Score that ranges between 300 and 850. They also have a Credit Tracker, which is a paid service you can subscribe to. With this service, you are entitled to a copy of your Experian credit report along with your FICO score, email alerts for credit monitoring, and fraud resolution support.

The Three Major Credit Bureaus

TransUnion Credit Reports

Like Experian, you can go to AnnualCreditReport.com to receive your TransUnion credit report for free once per year. They also allow you to place a TransUnion fraud alert on your credit profile. If you think you've been a victim of fraud, you can contact the credit bureau, and this will prevent any accounts from being opened or your credit from being checked without your permission. TransUnion will then notify Experian and Equifax of the credit freeze placed on your account.

Also, with a paid subscription, you will be able to take advantage of TransUnion's credit monitoring service in addition to the ability to place the credit freeze on your credit file.

TransUnion scores also range from 300 to 850 and have many credit score categories ranging from bad to excellent. A bad TransUnion credit score is 550 and below, while an excellent TransUnion credit score would be 750 and up.

Equifax Credit Reports

Equifax also provides FICO and VantageScores and uses different scoring models to calculate your credit score. Similar to the others, the credit scores will range between 300 and 850.

Equifax also provides a monthly subscription service which allows for credit monitoring that provides you with your credit scores, credit reports, credit freezes, and other alerts.

It's a good idea to review your credit reports from all three credit reporting agencies for the finer details influencing your credit scores, as well as to monitor your scores for any sudden changes, as these can be a sign of identity theft.

Knowing your credit scores will help provide you with a better idea of what types of terms and conditions you may qualify for on any lines of credit or loans from financial institutions. Also, understanding the role each reporting agency has will give you the upper hand when it comes to your rights and the security of your credit accounts with each bureau.

Experian unlocks the power of data to create opportunities for consumers, businesses, and society during life's big moments: from buying a home or car, to sending a child to college, to growing a business exponentially by connecting it with new customers.

We gather, analyze, and process data in ways others can't. We help individuals take financial control and access financial services, businesses make smarter decisions and thrive, lenders lend more responsibly, and organizations prevent identity fraud and crime.

For more than 125 years, we've helped consumers and clients prosper, and economies and communities flourish—and we're not done.

Our 17,000 people in 37 countries believe the possibilities for you, and our world, are growing. We're investing in new technologies, talented people, and innovation so we can help create a better tomorrow. Learn more at www.experianplc.com.

Chapter Seven:

Credit Fraud/Identity Theft

Identity Theft

Identity theft is the deliberate use of someone else's identity, usually as a method to gain a financial advantage or obtain credit and benefits in the other person's name, and perhaps to the other person's disadvantage or loss.

What Should I Do if I Think My Identity Has Been Stolen?

If you become a victim of identity theft or even suspect that you might be a victim, take immediate action.

1. Contact one of the credit reporting agencies' fraud alert departments and place a fraud alert on your credit report. This prevents identity thieves from opening accounts in your name. Many credit card companies offer no-cost fraud protection where you will not be held financially responsible for charges made to your account by thieves who steal your personal information.

TIPS & ADVICE

EUROPOL
EC3 European Cybercrime Centre

To Prevent Identity Theft Happening To You

Identity theft is big business! Personal and financial data stolen online is sold in the underground economy, and is misused by criminal organisations all over the world. Protecting your data doesn't just save you the inconvenience of having to change your passwords and credit cards, by making it more difficult for criminals to obtain your details you can help in the fight against organized crime and terrorism.

DOS ✓

BE AWARE. Treat unsolicited emails or pages asking for personal information with suspicion, particularly those claiming to be from banks and credit card companies. A quick web search can tell you if the email you've received is a known scam. Remember that you can always check with your bank or credit card company if the email you received is really from them.

UPDATE YOUR SOFTWARE REGULARLY. Many malware infections are the result of criminals exploiting bugs in software (web browsers, operating systems, common tools, etc.). Keeping these up to date can help to keep you safe.

USE ANTI-VIRUS SOFTWARE. Anti-virus (AV) software can help keep your computer free of the most common malware. You can easily find many free options of such software. Always check downloaded files with AV software. Do not install programs or applications on your computer if you don't know where they have come from.

DON'TS ✗

CLICK ON ATTACHMENTS AND LINKS WITHOUT KNOWING THEIR TRUE ORIGIN. What looks like a harmless video or image can actually be malicious software designed to steal your data. Even opening a spam email can put your address on a spammer's future hit list.

GIVE AWAY MORE INFORMATION THAN NECESSARY. Your bank and credit card provider already know your PIN number and address. They don't need you to tell them via email, phone or a web page.

ACCESS ONLINE BANKING FROM SHARED OR PUBLIC COMPUTERS. You never know what might be lurking on their hard drives.

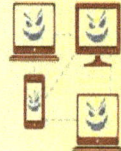

2. You must call one of the credit reporting agencies as soon as you possibly can, even if you aren't 100 percent sure your identity has been stolen but may only think it has been. Tell the agency you think your identity has been stolen. The agency will ask you to verify your identity with your Social Security number, name, address, and possibly other personal information.

3. One call does it all. The credit reporting agency you contacted must contact the other two. Each agency will place a fraud alert on their version of your credit report. For the next n days, your creditors and other businesses that want to offer you credits will see the alert on your credit report. If anyone asks for credit in your name, the appropriate lender will contact you to verify your identity and find out if you asked for credit.

Equifax Fraud Department

Call 1-800-525-6285

Visit www.equifax.com

Experian Fraud Department

Call 1-888-397-3742

Visit www.experian.com

TransUnion Fraud Department

Call 1-800-680-7289

Visit http://www.transunion.com

4. Contact your lenders, banks, and insurance companies and let them know the situation. Ask to close accounts. Open new ones with new personal identification numbers (PINs) and passwords.

5. Victims of identity theft are entitled to a free credit report. Wait about a month before you request it. Some activity may take a while to show up on your report. Listed are the changes to observe.

   ➢ Personal information that has changed: your name, date of birth, Social Security number, address, and employer
   ➢ Inquiries from companies you didn't contact
   ➢ Accounts you didn't open
   ➢ Debts on your accounts you can't explain

6. File a police report—it is proof of the crime. If the credit reporting agencies need to investigate fraudulent activity on your report, they will need this police report.

7. Periodically check your credit reports over the next year to make sure no new fraudulent activity has occurred.

8. Work with the credit reporting agencies to remove fraudulent activities from your credit report.

Consumer Information

Federal Trade Commission

https://www.consumer.ftc.gov/topics/identity-theft

USA.gov

https://www.usa.gov/identity-theft

If you are an identity theft victim, FACTA gives you the right to:

- ➤ **Place a "Fraud Alert" in Your Credit Reports.** An alert makes potential creditors wary of credit applications and inquiries in your name, protecting you from additional fraud. This can be short-term or long-term, anywhere from ninety days to seven years.

- ➤ **Receive Free Copies of Your Credit Reports.** Check the documents for signs of fraud, such as an unauthorized line of credit or a change of address.

- ➤ **Request and Obtain Copies of Documents Related to Fraudulent Dealings.** You may be required to show proof of identity theft, such as a police report.

- ➤ **Request and Obtain Relevant Information from Debt Collectors.** This includes details of the debt, such as the creditor and amount due.

➤ **Request a "Block" on Information Resulting from Identity Theft.** When supplied with adequate proof, credit reporting agencies can prevent an identity thief's actions from appearing on your credit report and negatively affecting your credit score.

➤ **Request Businesses to Not Report Information Related to Your Identity Theft.** Once you provide proof of identity theft, the involved businesses can stop reporting the false information to credit reporting agencies, preventing negative effects to your credit report.

Chapter Eight:

Credit Fraud Prevention

Preventing Fraud

You can take steps now to protect yourself from credit fraud. Learn the warning signs and get the information you need to prevent credit fraud and identity theft. By being informed about the sources that credit thieves use to steal personal information, you can better protect yourself from becoming a victim.

The earlier you discover credit fraud, the better. If you believe you are a victim of fraud, there are steps you can take to protect your credit.

Learn how to prevent and respond to identity theft. Below are immediate step-by-step instructions and tips to take for recovery.

➢ **Fraud Alerts**: Fraud alert messages notify potential credit grantors to verify your identification before extending credit in your name in case someone is using your information without your consent.

➢ **Security Freezes**: A security freeze is designed to prevent credit, loans, and services from being approved in your name without your consent but may also delay or interfere with or prohibit the timely approval of any subsequent requests or application you make regarding new credit, loans, or services.

Tips to Protect Your Identity Online

Identity theft is on the rise, with the number of victims steadily climbing year after year, according to a Javelin research study. Since the rise in personal technology and social media leads to increased vulnerability in users' personal information, it is the consumer's job to stay aware and take preventative action. Here are some tips on how to prevent becoming a victim of identity theft:

CREATE STRONG PASSWORDS

****

Make them long, include special characters, change often and don't use the same one for multiple accounts

PROTECT YOUR SMARTPHONE

Don't keep any personal information on your phone, especially without a password lock

KNOW WHAT INFO YOU SHARE

Know the personal information you're sharing on social media and manage your account's privacy settings

MOST POPULAR PASSWORDS OF 2011

1. Password
2. 123456
3. 12345678
4. abc123
5. qwerty
6. monkey
7. letmein
8. DRAGON
9. 111111
10. baseball

SMARTPHONE USERS

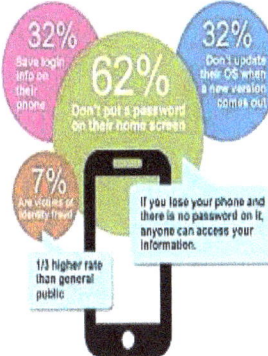

32% Save login info on their phone

32% Don't update their OS when a new version comes out

62% Don't put a password on their home screen

7% Are victims of identity fraud

1/3 higher rate than general public

If you lose your phone and there is no password on it, anyone can access your information.

PEOPLE WITH PUBLIC PROFILES

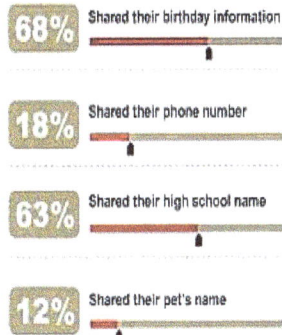

68% Shared their birthday information

18% Shared their phone number

63% Shared their high school name

12% Shared their pet's name

What is Credit Fraud?

According to credit fraud statistics, credit fraud and identity theft are a small part of overall credit card spending in the United States. Losses due to default far exceed those caused by fraud. However, if credit fraud or identity theft happens to you, it can be overwhelming. Victims may be protected financially, but they are forced to experience major inconvenience. Ultimately, we all pay for credit card fraud in terms of higher prices, higher interest rates, and extra inconvenience.

Types of Credit Fraud

Credit fraud is a broad term for the use of a credit card (or any comparable type of credit) to buy goods and services or evade payment. Credit fraud includes:

➢ **Identity theft:** The unauthorized use of personal identification information to commit credit fraud or other crimes

➢ **Identity assumption:** Long-term victimization of identification information

➢ **Fraud spree:** Unauthorized charges on existing accounts

Sources of Credit Fraud

Just as there are various types of credit fraud, there also are different ways that credit thieves gather your personal information:

- ➢ Using lost or stolen credit cards
- ➢ Stealing from your mailbox
- ➢ Looking over your shoulder during transactions
- ➢ Going through your trash
- ➢ Sending unsolicited emails
- ➢ Making false telephone solicitations
- ➢ Looking at personal records

Discovering Fraud

There are several warning signs that credit fraud may be occurring:

- ➢ Your credit report contains inquiries or information about accounts that you did not open
- ➢ Strange charges show up on billing statements
- ➢ Bills arrive from unknown or unfamiliar sources
- ➢ You receive calls from creditors or collection agencies

More Resources for Responding to Different Types of Fraud

- ➤ Driver's license number fraud: Notify your state's Department of Motor Vehicles
- ➤ Social Security number used to commit identity theft: Contact the Federal Trade Commission at 1 (877) 438-4338
- ➤ Passport used in identity theft: Contact the U.S. State Department, Passport Services Department
- ➤ Mail fraud: Visit the U.S. Postal Service® Website, Government Services

Victim Assistance

We suggest you follow a four-step process if you notice something unfamiliar or suspicious on one of your accounts or if someone accesses your bank account or commits any type of fraudulent activity using your identity.

Step 1: Contact the National Consumer Assistance Center

An initial security alert can be immediately added to your credit file. It alerts creditors to confirm your identity before extending credit. Once an alert is added, your name will be removed from prescreened credit solicitation lists.

Remember: An alert may prevent you from being approved for new credit or you may be asked to provide identifying information!

Once you add your 90-day fraud alert, you will have the option to get your free report on the confirmation screen.

The alert will be shared with the other national credit reporting companies so they can add the alert to their credit files.

Step 2: Review Complimentary Credit Report or Order Report

Review your consumer disclosure for fraudulent data and call the special telephone number listed on the credit report.

Step 3: Credit Bureaus Investigate

Credit bureaus will verify the information that the consumer alleges as fraudulent with the creditors or data furnishers. Upon receipt of a valid police report or valid state approved identity theft form, block alleged fraudulent information from view by creditors and other users of the report. It allows you to continue to be credit-active without being penalized for any fraudulent information on your report (Submit Police Report or Proof Documents Online).

Credit bureaus employ special system procedures and matching criteria to ensure that fraudulent data is removed as soon as possible.

Step 4: Fraudulent Data Is Removed

Credit bureaus must complete an investigation within 30 days, or 45 days if the information on an annual credit report is disputed.

The data contributor is asked to verify the information it reported with its records.

Once the response is received, the consumer will be notified of the results of the investigation.

The Difference Between a Fraud Alert and a Security Freeze

A fraud alert or initial security alert is a statement that appears on your credit report. This statement notifies creditors that they should contact you before granting credit in your name.

A security freeze prohibits anyone from accessing your credit report. Your credit file must be unfrozen for any creditors to access your credit. You can freeze or unfreeze your credit report at any time with your PIN or by verifying your personal information and answering a few questions.

Resources

If you suspect you are a victim of identity theft, here is some important contact information that can help you respond:

Experian Fraud Division

1 (888) 397 3742

Equifax Fraud Division

1 (800) 525 6285

TransUnion Fraud Division

1 (800) 680 7289

Driver's license number fraud

Notify your state's Department of Motor Vehicles

Social Security number used to commit identity theft

Notify the Federal Trade Commission at 1 (877) ID THEFT or 1 (877) 438 4338

Passport used in identity theft

Contact the U.S. State Department, Passport Services Department

Mail fraud

Visit the U.S. Postal Service® Website, Government Services

Under the Fair Credit Reporting Act, you have a right to:

➢ Access Your Credit Report: The act requires credit reporting agencies to provide you with any information in your credit file upon request once a year. You must have proper identification. You have the right to a free copy of your credit report within fifteen days of your request.

➢ Protected Access: The act limits access to your file to those with a valid need. That would usually be banks, insurance companies, employers, landlords, or others doing business that involves offering credit. You also have the right to know who has requested your credit report in the last year, or for employment-related requests in the last two years.

➢ Accurate Reporting: If inaccurate information is discovered in your file, the consumer reporting agency must examine the disputed information, usually within 30 days. If the inaccurate information cannot be verified, the consumer reporting agency has a responsibility to remove it. If you are not able to clear up the matter, you are allowed to add a statement to your credit file explaining the situation.

- Has Outdated Information Been Removed: Negative information must be removed from your file after seven years. Bankruptcy, however, may remain on record for ten years, and criminal record information can remain indefinitely.

- Maintain Medical Information Privacy: You are protected from having medical information in a consumer report, as creditors are prohibited from obtaining or using medical information when making a credit decision.

- Limit Unsolicited Credit Offers: The law allows you to request to have your name and address removed from unsolicited prescreened offer lists for credit and insurance. To opt-out of such correspondence, call (888) 5-OPTOUT or (888)-567-8688.

- Protect Your Personal Account Numbers: Businesses are not permitted to publish full credit card numbers on receipts. The law also allows you to protect your Social Security number by having it truncated on your credit report.

- Receive Notification of Possible Negative Information: You have the right to be notified of any financial institution submits, or plans to submit negative information to a credit reporting agency. This information may be included in a billing statement or a notice of default.

➤ Seek Damages: You have the right to sue and seek damages in a state or federal court from anyone, such as a consumer reporting agency or a user of consumer reports who violates the Fair Credit Reporting Act.

➤ Know When Your Credit Report Is Being Used Against You: If you are denied credit, insurance, or employment because of your credit report, you can ask for the specific reason for the denial.

➤ Know Your Credit Scores: You have a unique credit score with each credit bureau, which you can request. In some cases, you may be required to pay for this information.

Glossary

Account: An account is a record in the general ledger that is used to collect and store debit and credit amounts. An amount of money deposited with a bank, as in checking or savings.

Account Classification: Most General Ledger accounts have a classification; all assets, liabilities, and equity accounts *must* have a classification. The classification is used for several purposes:

- Asset
- Liability
- Equity
- Revenue
- Expenses

Account Condition: Indicates the present state of the account, but does not indicate the payment history of the account that led to the current state (i.e., open, paid, charge off, repossession, settled, foreclosed, etc).

Accounts in Good Standing: Credit items that have a positive status and should reflect favorably on your creditworthiness.

Account Number: The unique number assigned by a creditor to identify your account with them. Experian removes several digits of each account number on the credit report as a fraud prevention measure.

Account Rating: There are standard codes set by the credit reporting industry, which the creditors use when they provide this information to the credit bureaus. The credit bureaus only report what is provided to them and do not determine the rating. Here is a breakdown of the ratings:

> ➢ A new account that is "too new to rate" is rated 0.
> ➢ An account that is paid on time and is the best rating is "pays as agreed" and rated 1.
> ➢ An account 30 days late, which is considered 30 to 59 days past due, is rated 2.
> ➢ An account 60 days late, which is 60 to 89 days past due, is rated 3.
> ➢ An account 90 days late, which is 90 to 119 days past due, is rated 4.

- ➤ An account 120 days late, which is 120 to 149 days past due, is rated 5.
- ➤ Regular payments agreed upon under a wage earner plan is rated 6.
- ➤ Repossession is rated 8.
- ➤ Bad debt or a collection is rated 9.

Adjustment: Percentage of the debt that is to be repaid to the credit grantors in a Chapter 13 bankruptcy.

AKA: Also Known As.

Annual Fee: Credit card issuers often, but not always, require you to pay a special charge once a year for the use of their service, usually between $15 and $55.

Annual Percentage Rate (APR): A measure of how much interest credit will cost you, expressed as an annual percentage.

Authorized User: A person permitted by a credit cardholder to charge goods and services on the cardholder's account but who is not responsible for the repayment of the debt. The account displays on the credit reports of the cardholder as well as the authorized user. If you wish to have your name permanently removed as an authorized user on an account, you will need to notify the credit grantor.

Balloon Payments: A loan with a balloon payment requires that a single, lump-sum payment be made at the end of the loan.

Bankruptcy Code: Federal laws governing the conditions and procedures under which persons claiming an inability to repay their debts can seek relief.

Capacity: Factor in determining creditworthiness. Capacity is assessed by weighing a borrower's earning ability and the likelihood of continuing income against the amount of debt the borrower carries at the time the credit application is made. While capacity may be considered in a credit decision, the credit report does not contain information about earning ability or the likelihood of continuing income.

Certificate of Deposit: A certificate issued by a bank to a person depositing money for a specified length of time.

Chapter 7 Bankruptcy: Chapter of the Bankruptcy Code that provides for court administered liquidation of the assets of a financially troubled individual or business.

Chapter 11 Bankruptcy: Chapter of the Bankruptcy Code that is usually used for the reorganization of a financially troubled business. Used as an alternative to liquidation under Chapter 7. The U.S. Supreme Court has confirmed that an individual may also use Chapter 11.

Chapter 12 Bankruptcy: Chapter of the Bankruptcy Code adopted to address the financial crisis of the nation's farming community. Cases under this chapter are administered similar to Chapter 11 cases, but with special protections to meet the special conditions of family farm operations.

Chapter 13 Bankruptcy: Chapter of the Bankruptcy Code in which debtors repay debts according to a plan accepted by the debtor, the creditors, and the court. Plan payments usually come from the debtor's future income and are paid to creditors through the court system and the bankruptcy trustee.

Charge Off: The action of transferring accounts deemed uncollectible to a category such as bad debt or loss. Collectors will usually continue to solicit payments, but the accounts are no longer considered part of a company's receivable or profit picture.

Civil Action: Any court action against a consumer to regain money for someone else. Usually, it will be a wage assignment, child support judgment, small claims judgment, or a civil judgment.

Civil Judgement: A ruling made by a court during a lawsuit. In many cases, people have judgments because of unpaid collections or other financial obligations. These judgements show up on your credit report as a public record placed there by the credit bureaus.

Claim Amount: The amount awarded in a court action.

Closed Date: The date an account was closed.

Co-maker: A creditworthy co-maker is sometimes required in situations where an applicant's qualifications are marginal. A co-maker is legally responsible to repay the charges in the joint account agreement.

Consumer Reporting Agency or Credit Bureau: A collection agency that gathers account information from various creditors and provides that information to a consumer reporting agency in the United States, a credit reference agency in the United Kingdom, a credit reporting body in Australia, a credit information company (CIC) in India, Special Accessing Entity in the Philippines, and also to private lenders.

Cosigner: Person who pledges in writing as part of a credit contract to repay the debt if the borrower fails to do so. The account displays on both the borrower's and the cosigner's credit report.

Credit Analysis: Credit analysis is a type of analysis an investor or bond portfolio manager performs on companies or other debt issuing entities to measure the entity's ability to meet its debt obligations. The credit analysis seeks to identify the appropriate level of default risk associated with investing in that particular entity.

Credit Capacity: This is how much credit you can handle. In deciding whether you qualify for a particular loan, your income is considered along with any other expenses and debts you may have.

Credit Grantor: Another term used to describe your credit card issuer. The company has granted credit to you.

Credit History: A record of a borrower's responsible repayment of debts. A credit report is a record of the borrower's credit history from several sources, including banks, credit card companies, collection agencies, and governments.

Credit Items: Information reported by current or past creditors.

Credit Limit/Line of Credit: In open-end credit, the maximum amount a borrower can draw upon or the maximum that an account can show as outstanding.

Credit Reference: This is information, the name of an individual, or the name of an organization that can provide details about an individual's past track record with credit.

Credit rating agencies provide credit references for companies while credit bureaus provide credit references for individuals.

Credit Report: Confidential report on a consumer's payment habits as reported by their creditors to a consumer credit reporting agency. The agency provides the information to credit grantors who have a permissible purpose under the law to review the report.

Credit Scoring: A tool used by credit grantors to provide an objective means of determining risks in granting credit. Credit scoring increases efficiency and timely response in the credit granting process. Credit scoring criteria are set by the credit grantor.

Credit Stability: An intrinsic characteristic of credit or a sector and should not be confused with rating stability. Ratings represent a forward-looking view on creditworthiness, and they migrate in line with any change in our view on credit conditions or expectations.

Creditworthiness: The ability of a consumer to receive favorable consideration and approval for the use of credit from an establishment to which they applied.

Date Filed: The date that a public record was awarded.

Date Opened: On the credit report; indicates the date an account was opened.

Date of Status: The date the creditor last updated the account. This date does not affect how long an account remains on the report and should not be confused with the "Original Delinquency Date."

Date Resolved: The completion date or satisfaction date of a public record item.

Defendant: An individual, company, or institution sued or accused in a court of law.

Delinquent: Accounts classified according to the time past due. Common classifications are 30, 60, 90, and 120 days past due. Special classifications also include charge-off, repossession, transferred, etc.

Discharge: Granted by the court to release a debtor from most of his debts that were included in a bankruptcy. Any debts not included in the bankruptcy—alimony, child support, liability for willful and malicious conduct, and certain student loans— cannot be discharged.

Disclosure: Providing the consumer with his or her credit history as required by the FCRA.

Dismissed: When a consumer files a bankruptcy, the judge may decide to not allow the consumer to continue with the bankruptcy. If the judge rules against the petition, the bankruptcy is known as dismissed.

Dispute: If a consumer believes an item of information on their credit report is inaccurate or incomplete, they may challenge or dispute the item.

Docket Number: In general, courts assign each newly filed action with a docket number, which often refers to the year in which the case was commenced followed by a sequential reference number, and sometimes includes letters or numbers indicating the type (civil, criminal, family court, etc.) or location of filing and/or the initials.

ECOA: Standard abbreviation for Equal Credit Opportunity Act. **End-user**: The business that receives the report for decision-making purposes that meet the permissible purpose requirements of the FCRA.

Equal Credit Opportunity Act (ECOA): Federal law, which prohibits creditors from discriminating against credit applicants based on sex, marital status, race, color, religion, age, and/or receipt of public assistance.

Equifax: One of the three national credit reporting agencies headquartered in Atlanta, GA. The other two are Experian and TransUnion.

Experian: One of the three national credit reporting agencies with U.S. headquarters in Costa Mesa, CA. The other two are Equifax and TransUnion.

Fair Credit Billing Act: Federal legislation that provides a specific error resolution procedure to protect credit card customers from making payments on inaccurate billings.

Fair Credit and Charge Card Disclosure Act: Amendments to the Truth in Lending Act that require the disclosure of the costs involved in credit card plans that are offered by mail, telephone, or applications distributed to the general public.

Fair Credit Reporting Act (FCRA): Federal legislation governing the actions of credit reporting agencies.

Fair Debt Collection Practices Act (FDCPA): Federal legislation prohibiting abusive and unfair debt collection practices.

Finance Charge: Amount of interest. Finance charges are usually included in the monthly payment total.

First Reported: The date when the first account status was reported by the account holder.

Fixed-Rate: An annual percentage rate that does not change.

Foreclosure: A legal process in which a lender attempts to recover the balance of a loan from a borrower who has stopped making payments to the lender by forcing the sale of the asset used as the collateral for the loan.

Grace Period: The period you have to pay a bill in full and avoid interest charges.

Guarantor: Person responsible for paying a bill.

High Balance: The highest amount that you have owed on an account to date.

Installment Credit: Credit accounts in which the debt is divided into amounts to be paid successively at specified intervals.

Interest: Money paid regularly at a particular rate for the use of money lent, or for delaying the repayment of a debt.

Investigation: The process a consumer credit reporting agency goes through to verify credit report information disputed by a consumer. The credit grantor who supplied the information is contacted and asked to review the information and report back;

they will tell the credit reporting agency that the information is accurate as it appears, or correct information to update the report.

Investigative Consumer Reports: These are consumer reports that are usually done for background checks, security clearances, and other sensitive jobs. An investigative consumer report might contain information obtained from a credit report, but it is more comprehensive than a credit report. It contains subjective material on an individual's character, habits, and mode of living, which is obtained through interviews of associates. Experian does not provide investigative consumer reports.

Involuntary Bankruptcy: A petition filed by certain credit grantors to have a debtor judged bankrupt. If bankruptcy is granted, it is known as involuntary bankruptcy.

Item-specific Statement: Offers an explanation about a particular trade or public record item on your report, and it displays with that item on the credit report.

Judgment Granted: The determination of a court upon matters submitted to it. A final determination of the rights of the parties involved in the lawsuit.

Last Reported: On the credit report; the date the creditor last reported information about the account.

Liability: The state of being responsible for something, especially by law.

Liability Amount: Amount for which you are legally obligated to a creditor.

Lien: Legal document used to create a security interest in another's property. A lien is often given as security for the payment of a debt. A lien can be placed against a consumer for failure to pay the city, county, state, or federal government money that is owed. It means that the consumer's property is being used as collateral during repayment of the money that is owed.

Line of Credit: In open-end credit, the maximum amount a borrower can draw upon or the maximum that an account can show as outstanding.

Loan: A thing that is borrowed, especially a sum of money that is expected to be paid back with interest.

Location Number: The book and page number on which the item is filed in the court records.

Manner of Payment (MOP): The way that a buyer chooses to compensate the seller for a good or service that is also acceptable to the seller.

Typical payment methods used in a modern business context include cash, checks, credit or debit cards, money orders, bank transfers, and online payment services such as PayPal.

Non-Verification: Cannot compare two or more items, or the use of supplementary tests, to ensure the accuracy, correctness, or truth of the information.

Notice of Results: If your investigation results in information being updated or deleted, you may request that corrected information in your credit history to eligible credit grantors and employers who reviewed your information within a specific period. If your investigation does not result in a change to your credit history, results will not be sent to other lenders.

Obsolescence: A term used to describe how long negative information should stay in a credit file before it's not relevant to the credit granting decision. The FCRA has determined the obsolescence period to be ten years in the case of bankruptcy and seven years in all other instances. Unpaid tax liens may remain indefinitely; although, Experian removes them after fifteen years.

Original Amount: The original amount owed to a creditor.

Original Delinquency Date: The date an account first became delinquent and after which it was never again brought current.

Payment History: A payment history is an indication for lenders and creditors whether an individual is a lending risk due to a history of late or missed payments.

Payment Status: Reflects the previous history of the account, including any delinquencies or derogatory conditions occurring during the previous seven years (i.e., current account, delinquent 30, the current was 60, redeemed repossession, charge-off, now paying, etc.).

Personal Information: Information on your credit report associated with your records that has been reported to creditors and other sources. It may include name variations, your driver's license number, Social Security number variations, your date or year of birth, your spouse's name, your employers, your telephone numbers, and information about your residence.

Personal Statement: You may request that a general explanation about the information on your report be added to your report. The statement remains for two years and displays to anyone who reviews your credit information.

Petition: If a consumer files a bankruptcy, but a judge has not yet ruled that it can proceed, it is known as bankruptcy petitioned.

Plaintiff: One who initially brings legal action against another (defendant) seeking a court decision.

Potentially Negative Items: Any potentially negative credit items or public records that may affect your creditworthiness as viewed by creditors.

Primary User: The user that initially created the account. Primary users will be able to edit their information as well as the information of secondary users.

Recent Balance: The most recent balance owed on an account as reported by the creditor.

Recent Payment: The most recent amount paid on an account as reported by the creditor.

Released: This means that a lien has been satisfied in full.

Repossession: A process where an auto lender can take back possession of your vehicle, sometimes without warning you or having permission from the court. Repossession typically occurs after you've fallen behind on your auto loan payments.

Report Number: A number that uniquely identifies each personal credit report. This number displays on your credit report and should always be used as a reference.

Reported Since: On the credit report; the date the creditor started reporting.

Request an Investigation: If you believe that information on your report is inaccurate, we will ask the sources of the information to check their records at no cost to you. Incorrect information will be corrected; information that cannot be verified will be deleted. Experian cannot remove accurate information. An investigation may take up to thirty days. When it is complete, we'll send you the results.

Request for Your Credit History: When a credit grantor, direct marketer, or potential employer requests information from a consumer's credit report, an inquiry is shown on the report. Grantors only see credit inquiries generated by other grantors as a result of an application of some kind, while consumers see all listed inquiries including prescreened and direct marketing offers, as well as employment inquiries. According to the Fair Credit Reporting Act, credit grantors with a permissible purpose may inquire about your credit information before your consent. This section also includes the date of the inquiry and how long the inquiry will remain on your report.

Responsibility: Indicates who is responsible for an account; can be single, joint, co-signer, etc.

Revolving Account: Credit automatically available up to a predetermined maximum limit so long as a customer makes regular payments.

Risk Scoring Models: A numerical determination of a consumer's creditworthiness. A tool used by credit grantors to predict the future payment behavior of a consumer.

Satisfied: If the consumer has paid all of the money the court says he owes, the public record item is satisfied.

Season Trade Line: A line of credit that the borrower has held open in good standing for a long period, typically at least two years. The "seasoned" part simply implies that the account is aged or that it has an established history.

Secured Credit: Loan for which some form of acceptable collateral, such as a house or automobile has been pledged.

Security: Real or personal property that a borrower pledges for the term of a loan. Should the borrower fail to repay, the creditor may take ownership of the property by following legally mandated procedures.

Security Alert: Statement that is added once Experian is notified that a consumer may be a victim of fraud. It remains on file for ninety days and requests that a creditor request proof of identification before granting credit in that person's name.

Service Credit: Agreements with service providers. You receive goods, such as electricity and services, apartment rentals, and health club memberships, with the agreement that you will pay for them each month. Your contract may require payments for a specific number of months, even if you stop the service.

Settle: Reach an agreement with a lender to repay only part of the original debt.

Shared Account: An account with two people listed as owners.

Source: The business or organization that supplied certain information that appears on the credit report.

Status: On the credit report, this indicates the current status or state of the account.

Statute: A written law passed by a legislative body.

Subscriber: A person who pays to receive or access a service.

Tax Form 12277: The tax screwup that can destroy your credit. Form 12277 is the "Application for Withdrawal of Filed Form 668 (Y), Notice of Federal Tax Lien." The form has been available to taxpayers for years, but originally the stipulations to withdraw a tax lien by the IRS were so stringent, few people ever succeeded.

Tax Lien: A lien imposed by law upon a property to secure the payment of taxes. A tax lien may be imposed for delinquent taxes owed on real property or personal property, or as a result of failure to pay income taxes or other taxes.

Terms: This refers to the debt repayment terms of your agreement with a creditor, such as sixty months, forty-eight months, etc.

Third-Party Collectors: Collectors who are under contract to collect debts for a credit department or credit company; a collection agency.

Tradeline: Entry by a credit grantor to a consumer's credit history maintained by a credit reporting agency. A tradeline describes the consumer's account status and activity. Tradeline information includes names of companies where the applicant has accounts, dates accounts were opened, credit limits, types of accounts, balances owed, and payment histories.

Transaction Fees: Fees charged for certain use of your credit line. For example, to get a cash advance from an ATM.

TransUnion: One of three national credit reporting agencies. The other two are Experian and Equifax.

Trustee: A person or member of a board given control or powers of administration of property in trust with a legal obligation to administer it solely for the purposes specified.

Truth in Lending Act: Title I of the Consumer Protection Act. It requires that most categories of lenders disclose the annual interest rate, the total dollar cost, and other terms of loans and credit sales.

Undesignated Account: No status was reported by the creditor reporting the account information.

Unsecured Credit: Credit for which no collateral has been pledged. Loans made under this arrangement are sometimes called signature loans; in other words, a loan is granted based only on the customer's word through signing an agreement that the loan amount will be paid.

Vacated: Indicates a judgment that was rendered void or set aside.

Variable Rate: An annual percentage rate that may change over time as the prime lending rate varies or according to your contract with the lender.

Verification: Verifying whether data in a credit report is correct or not. Initiated by consumers when they question some information in their file. Credit reporting agencies will accept authentic documentation from the consumer that will help in the verification.

Victim Statement: A statement that can be added to a consumer's credit report to alert credit grantors that a consumer's identification has been used fraudulently to obtain credit. The statement requests the credit grantor to contact the consumer by telephone before issuing credit. It remains on file for seven years unless the consumer requests that it be removed.

Voluntary Bankruptcy: If a consumer files bankruptcy on their own, it is known as voluntary bankruptcy.

Wage Assignment: A signed agreement by a buyer, or borrower, permitting a creditor to collect a certain portion of the debtor's wages from an employer in the event of default.

Withdrawn: This means a decision was made not to pursue a bankruptcy, a lien, etc., after court documents have been filed.

Writ of Replevin: Legal document issued by a court authorizing repossession of security

Other Books by Chayo Briggs

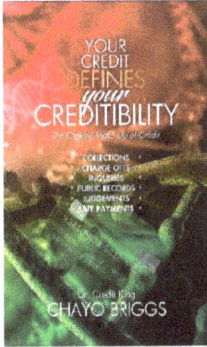

Your Credit Defines Your Creditibility

In the second edition of Your Credit Defines Your Credibility Chayo Briggs discusses a pathway to understanding what contributes to an excellent credit rating. We know such issues are daunting, but you may need to borrow money from a lender, so it's important to know how credit scores are calculated. American's have faced uncertain times over the last year with the pandemic, making the need to establish a good credit score even more important.

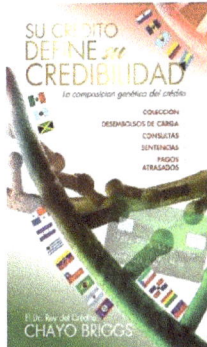

Su crédito define su credibilidad: La composición genética del crédito

Como inversor inmobiliario de gran éxito durante más de dieciocho años, Briggs se ve impulsado a obtener los más altos estándares para sus clientes. Sus logros como orador motivador y autor publicado se desarrollaron a partir de su experiencia de vida. A través de estas habilidades excepcionales aprendió el arte de los ingresos pasivos. Chayo puede ayudar a sus clientes a lograr un futuro próspero, rompiendo las cadenas de las dificultades financieras.

Follow Me

Website: chayobriggs.com
Facebook: @ drchayobriggs
Instagram: @drchayobriggs
Twitter: @ chayote23

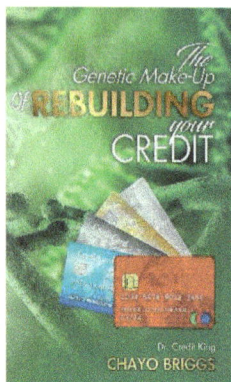

The Genetic Make-Up of Rebuilding Your Credit

The Genetic Make-Up of Rebuilding Your Credit focuses on the basics of establishing a solid credit resume. Chayo discusses the details on how to rebuild your credit with proven suggestions that will work overtime by using consistent good credit practices. The reasons people fall into credit problems are endless, but it's not a complete loss. Anyone can establish a good credit report if you know the necessary steps. Some topics discussed in the book are listed below: What is Credit?

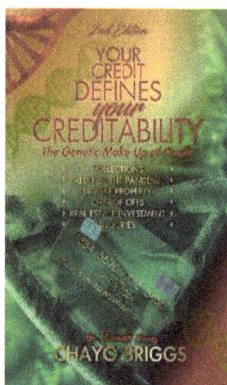

2nd Edition Your Credit Defines Your Creditability

In the second edition of Your Credit Defines Your Credibility Chayo Briggs discusses a pathway to understanding what contributes to an excellent credit rating. We know such issues are daunting, but you may need to borrow money from a lender, so it's important to know how credit scores are calculated. American's have faced uncertain times over the last year with the pandemic, making the need to establish a good credit score even more important.

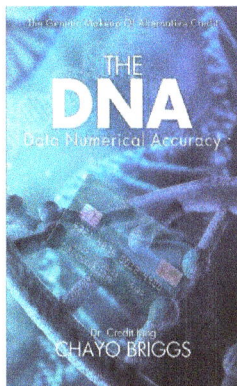

The (DNA) Data Numerical Accuracy

In '(DNA) Data Numerical Accuracy' the reader will learn credit is more than just borrowing money. Society is becoming heavily dependent on credit for daily necessities; it's not just for buying a house or car anymore. To a lender like an auto dealer or credit card company, credit is your reputation. Hence, a credit resume.

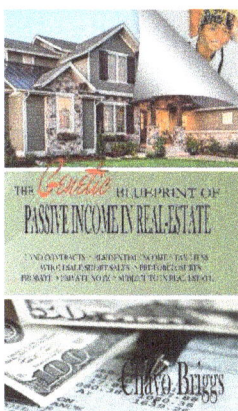

The Genetic Blueprint of Passive Income in Real-Estate

"The Genetic Blueprint of Passive Income in Real-Estate," is a great tool to instruct the reader on gaining long-term passive income. By increasing your monthly cash flow, you can start building retirement income faster, pay off debts, and, ultimately become financially independent. The number of investment opportunities is endless, but this book will focus on a few of the more preferable options. Such as Private Notes, Land Contracts, Residential Income, Wholesale/Short Sales, Pre-Foreclosures, Probate, Subject to.

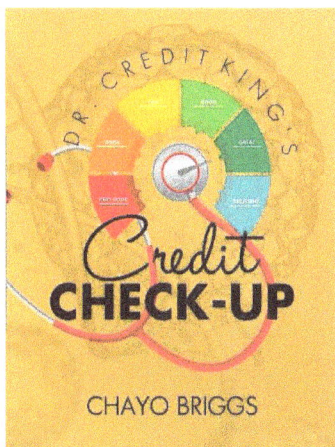

Dr. Credit King Check-Up

What is credit? This is a common question asked by many people around the world. Society is becoming heavily dependent on credit for daily necessities; it's not just for buying a house or car anymore. The job market or pay scales play a large role in someone's financial well-being. Even the ability to gain employment or rent an apartment is determined by a credit resume, and the impact of being denied credit can place a heavy burden on one's future

Dr. Credit King Credit App

The Dr. Credit King app helps guide users in repairing their credit score. It offers a variety of tools, to help users understand, improve, and avert credit threats, all right from your mobile device. Your Credit Defines Your Credibility, therefore, Dr. Credit King wants to make sure your credit is reported fairly and accurately.

Other app options allow online businesses to list their services free of charge. Plus, get the latest news on building good credit from Dr. Credit King/Chayo Briggs, or buy Dr. Credit King's books on iBooks to educate consumers on the fundamentals of credit and the importance of their creditability. Plus, connect to the Credit Blog for the latest articles to catch up on trending credit news, real-estate opportunities, learn how to grow passive income, and build wealth through different investments.

Not to mention, follow your Favorite Spotlight Credit Model and see how Dr. Credit King helped them with financial advice, as they moved forward with their modeling goals, acting, and financial careers. Subscribe on the website for the latest books from Dr. Credit King.

Bibliography

Board of Governors of the Federal Reserve System. "2016 Survey of Consumer Finances."

Federal Reserve Bank of New York. "The Center for Microeconomic Data", September 2020

Federal Reserve Bank of St. Louis. "Commercial Bank Interest Rate on Credit Card Plans, Accounts Assessed", August 2020

Peterson-Kaiser Health System Tracker. "Health System Dashboard", 2015

The Henry J. Kaiser Family Foundation. "Data Note: Americans' Challenges with Health Care Costs", March 2020

U.S. Bureau of Labor Statistics. "Consumer Price Index", September 2020

U.S. Census Bureau. "Families and Households", December 2016

www.ingramcontent.com/pod-product-compliance
Lightning Source LLC
Chambersburg PA
CBHW081815200326
41597CB00023B/4255